BEFORE
EQUAL SUFFRAGE

Recent Titles in
Contributions in Women's Studies

BEFORE EQUAL SUFFRAGE

*Women in Partisan Politics
from Colonial Times to 1920*

Robert J. Dinkin

Contributions in Women's Studies, Number 152

GREENWOOD PRESS
Westport, Connecticut • London

Library of Congress Cataloging-in-Publication Data

Dinkin, Robert J.
    Before equal suffrage : women in partisan politics from colonial
times to 1920 / Robert J. Dinkin.
        p.   cm. — (Contributions in women's studies, ISSN 0147–104X ;
no. 152)
    Includes bibliographical references and index.
    ISBN 0–313–29482–8 (alk. paper)
    1. Women in politics—United States—History.   I. Title.
II. Series.
HQ1236.5.U6D55   1995
305.42'0973—dc20   95–19321

British Library Cataloguing in Publication Data is available.

Library of Congress Catalog Card Number: 95–19321
ISBN: 0–313–29482–8
ISSN: 0147–104X

First published in 1995

Greenwood Press, 88 Post Road West, Westport, CT 06881
An imprint of Greenwood Publishing Group, Inc.

Printed in the United States of America

The paper used in this book complies with the
Permanent Paper Standard issued by the National
Information Standards Organization (Z39.48–1984).

10 9 8 7 6 5 4 3 2 1

Contents

Acknowledgments

This book took a long time from start to finish. The idea for it came to me during an NEH summer seminar on teaching women's history at Princeton University in 1980. It became a serious project over the next decade while I was doing research for another book, *Campaigning in America* (Greenwood Press, 1989), and noticed in the source material that women played a greater part in partisan politics than scholars have previously believed. Several persons have read parts or all of the manuscript and offered valuable criticism, including Lori Ginzberg of Pennsylvania State University, and Paula Baker of the University of Pittsburgh. I would also like to acknowledge the efforts of the staff at Greenwood Publishing Group, especially Cynthia Harris, Reference Editor, Desirée Bermani, Production Editor, and Betty Pessagno, Copyeditor, in enhancing the overall quality of the work. My wife, Roxane Head Dinkin, took time from her busy schedule to help improve the style of the final draft. Lastly, I must mention my daughter, Leslie Dinkin, who, during breaks from her studies at the University of California, Santa Cruz, put the entire manuscript on the word processor and subsequently inserted hundreds of additions and corrections at the request of her less than computer-literate father.

Introduction

Four decades ago, when Eleanor Roosevelt and Lorena Hickok collaborated on a pathbreaking book about women and partisan politics entitled *Ladies of Courage*, they began their story in 1920, the year American women finally acquired the vote on a national basis. Their brief description of political activity before that date dealt only with the woman suffrage movement. The implication seemed to be that members of the female sex did not really have any place in the partisan realm until after the suffrage amendment was ratified.[1] In the past fifteen years or so, a number of significant historical works have appeared which demonstrate that women did play a public role even prior to the long suffrage struggle, and over time they managed to exert a good deal of influence on the course of events despite their disenfranchisement. Such works tell of women's activism during the Revolutionary War era, and their efforts in behalf of social causes in the early nineteenth century. They discuss women's contribution to the abolitionist crusade and the post–Civil War temperance movement. They describe women's involvement in progressive reform and socialism in the late nineteenth and early twentieth centuries. Yet rarely do these studies, however important they are in delineating women's activities beyond the household, more than touch on their participation in partisan politics.[2]

Admittedly, a few of these writings and others cited later in this book do focus on certain aspects of women's partisan activity, starting with the second third of the nineteenth century. But the main emphasis in most of these monographs and related interpretive essays has been on the rather different political role of women than men and on women's merely marginal connection to mainstream politics. Paula Baker, in an influential article that appeared in the *American Historical Review*, wrote that partisan politics three-quarters of a century ago and earlier was essentially a male enterprise. "Partisan politics," she said, "united all white men regardless of class and other differences, and provided entertainment, a definition of manhood, and the basis for a male ritual." In this setting, she implied, women were not at all welcome. Baker goes on to state that in response to this pattern of exclusion women eventually formed their own separate (quasipolitical) interest organizations in the latter half of the nineteenth century, where they could pursue their own public agenda.[3] There is no recognition that some among their sex chose an alternative path and did on occasion attach themselves to one or another of the parties, working in concert with men, particularly at election time. Although Baker obliquely acknowledges some female participation in certain kinds of partisan events, she apparently sees it as having only minimal importance.

This last point is also stressed in a recent article by Michael McGerr, an authority on past American electioneering practices. Women, he states, were not barred entirely from partisan politics; there were always some tasks specifically assigned to them. During campaigns, it was female auxiliaries who "made food for rallies, sewed banners, and decorated meeting halls." In addition, they attended mass meetings and sometimes appeared in parades dressed up as symbolic figures like the Goddess of Liberty. But, concludes McGerr, this was the full extent of women's involvement. "They were allowed into the realm only to play typical feminine roles—to cook, to sew, and cheer men, and to symbolize virtue and beauty." In regard to the substance of politics, he contends, "men denied women the central experiences of the popular style: not only the ballot but also the experiences of mass mobilization."[4] In an essay published around the same time as McGerr's, historian Suzanne Lebsock presented an overview of women's political concerns in the four decades before 1920, and similarly proclaimed that female activists had only a minor part to play in the partisan sphere; "if they wanted influence [they] had no choice but to work through nonelectoral politics."[5]

It is not my intention here to summarily dismiss these statements. If one is compelled to draw general conclusions about the scope of the female political experience before 1920, those just cited are not terribly off the mark. After all, nonelectoral politics frequently commanded greater attention among women than the electoral variety, and those who ventured into the male-dominated partisan world found their opportunities quite limited. In most instances, women lacked the vote, which severely reduced their chances of exerting power. Relatively few could hold office at any level or have much say in regard to policy making. Rarely were they allowed to work on committees or attend conventions and caucuses. Few women active in campaigns took part in their overall planning or management. Within the organizational structure, they were usually relegated to minor positions that had little or no authority. Many indeed simply prepared food or cheered at rallies. Moreover, their partisan participation often occurred on a short-term or temporary basis—related to one issue or one election contest—rather than being permanent and ongoing as it was for the majority of men.

Yet portraying female partisans in previous epochs simply as ornamental figures without any influence does not provide a complete and accurate picture of either their status or their accomplishments. Even if women's activities were somewhat peripheral, it is clear that from the mid-nineteenth century onward they did more than just cook, sew, and cheer. Such women displayed more presence and had more impact, especially with their pen and voice, and in the realm of canvassing, than they have been given credit for. And if they did not hold the reins of power or receive the highest honors, then neither did most men.

Women added a feminine touch to political events—for example, waving handkerchiefs or presenting party banners at rallies. For the most part, however, they did not create a new female culture within the partisan framework, and their actions were not always separate and distinct. Although they sometimes formed partisan women's clubs and tried to work in ways that would not seem unladylike, they did in certain respects act in conjunction with men. During campaigns, women frequently attended mass meetings and other events together with the opposite sex. Women did, nonetheless, commonly possess a different attitude toward politics than men. They tended to be more selfless and more concerned about the public good, and generally they did not look so much for personal rewards. In fact, in many cases women entered the field of partisan politics in order to eliminate corruption or bring about some societal reform.

In contrast to the view of Paula Baker and several other historians, who see women as having created a political world totally apart from men, the reality was somewhat less easily defined. Many social reformers, though devoted mainly to nonpartisan humanitarian issues, often drifted into the partisan arena as the situation warranted; that is, they became more active when there seemed to be some advantage in backing a particular candidate or ticket. Of course, certain reformers shunned the idea of associating with parties because of the parties' sometimes questionable policies and shady dealings. Yet some believed that such organizations could be pushed in a positive direction, and they otherwise saw few alternatives to cooperative action with men in regard to achieving their societal goals. Interestingly, women in partisan politics tended to be most visible during the period of new party formation when the lines between a party and a social movement had not yet been fully drawn and when fledgling political groups seemed most in need of membership support.[6]

But whatever interest there may have been in reform, it is essential to note that the main focus of this volume is women and partisan politics—their association with the traditional domain of male-controlled parties—and not their affiliation with reform movements or other phases of public activity. (In fact, some types of partisan action, past and present, have been anything but public in nature.) Nevertheless, to understand the background as to how and why women moved into the partisan realm, it is sometimes necessary to discuss their involvement in certain kinds of nonpartisan political behavior. This is especially true for the Revolutionary and Early National periods, before a full-fledged party system had evolved. It is also vital for the post–Civil War era when various groups of reformers (e.g., temperance workers) later became attached to partisan organizations as a means of furthering their particular cause. In these instances, however, the main emphasis will be on the shift toward partisan activity and on the relationship with particular parties, not on the inner workings of the reform movement itself.

Yet it should be emphasized that not all women involved in partisan politics were concerned about reform. Although women were more likely than men to be interested in such matters, and quite a few of the most visible "female politicians" did follow reform agendas, a close connection with reform was by no means inevitable. Many women, particularly family members of male politicians, seem to have possessed a similar attitude toward politics as their menfolk, seeing it as a means to power and status or as an exciting form of competition they wished to enter. Indeed, some of them probably enjoyed the intrigue, the excitement, and the competitiveness of an electoral contest as much as the other sex. While barred from office and going to the polls, women like Jessie Benton Frémont and Mary Todd Lincoln often exerted considerable influence behind the scenes. And if they could not obtain high places for themselves, they could sometimes bask in the glory achieved by their husbands. The very fact that not all women saw politics from the standpoint of the reformer foreshadowed the development of female partisan behavior that would never be as homogeneous as the suffragists (or the antisuffragists) had predicted.[7]

As will be demonstrated throughout this volume, women's role in partisan politics was gradually on the upswing, both qualitatively and quantitatively. It did not have the relatively static character implied in the critical studies by Baker and McGerr cited earlier. In the century and a half before the suffrage amendment, women went from performing individual deeds to taking part in group actions, from waving handkerchiefs at parades and rallies to being speakers and publicists, and later creating partisan women's clubs and ultimately becoming voters in several western states. Of course, some things did not change very much. In every era, the term *female politician* was generally used in a derisive manner, and men opposed to women's political influence always played on fears of "petti-coat government." Politically active women had to hear time and again that their real place should be the kitchen and that by mixing in something that traditionally belonged to men they were creating friction and destroy-ing the home. Such women also bore the brunt of the blame if the "wrong" party or candidates were chosen to office. For example, after his side lost the Kansas state election to the Populists in 1890, a male Republican leader complained sarcastically, "As usual, there was a woman in the case . . . [Mary] Lease."[8] Regardless of the criticism, women became an ever-growing part of the political scene, and their full story needs to be told if we are to have a true understanding of how they reached their present position in the ever changing field of partisan politics.

ORGANIZATION OF THE BOOK

The book is divided into seven chapters, basically following a chrono-logical pattern. Chapter 1 discusses the colonial era and women's general exclusion from political life, especially their being denied the suffrage. It then describes the growth of female patriotic activity prior to and during the American Revolution, and the continuing exclusion of women from partisan politics in the postwar years except in New Jersey and in the case of a few extraordinary individuals such as Mercy Otis Warren and Abigail Adams.

Chapter 2 covers the Early National period through the late 1840s. It shows how most women in any way involved with politics under the first party system worked primarily behind the scenes; even in New Jersey women eventually lost the vote. Only in the 1830s and 1840s with the rise of the abolitionist movement and the emergence of the second party system did women become more numerous and openly involved in the partisan world. The election of 1840 served as a watershed for women's widening participation, though even then their actions were mainly peripheral—rid-ing in parades, cheering at rallies, hosting picnics and similar events. Yet some women were beginning to contribute in a more substantial way, particularly in the political aspects of such episodes as the Dorr Rebellion and the Lowell Mill strikes.

Chapter 3 illustrates women's continuing political participation before and during the Civil War, especially northern women who aided the rise of the Republican party and southern women who defended their region and promoted secession. It touches on the achievements of certain exceptional women such as publicists Anna Carroll and Harriet Beecher Stowe and the noted orator Anna Dickinson.

Chapter 4 looks at women's partisan behavior in the post–Civil War era, particularly the connection between the woman suffrage movement and the major parties, and the role played by major suffrage leaders in the partisan sphere. In addition, the chapter deals with those women in the postwar party struggle who were not at all committed to the quest for women's rights. Chapter 5 examines roughly the same time period—the late 1860s down to the mid-1890s—focusing on women who entered partisan politics through their association with the temperance movement, the Populist crusade, or the Socialist party. It tells how the phenomenon of women's involvement in minor reformist parties influenced the major parties to make better use of women in their own organizations, most notably through the formation of a network of partisan women's clubs. The achievements of J. Ellen Foster and the Women's National Republican Association are highlighted.

Chapter 6 traces the development of women voting, first in "partial suffrage" states in school board and municipal elections, and then in the four full suffrage states in the West. It also discusses women's partisan activities during the Progressive era. The last chapter assesses the link with partisan politics as women launched the final drive for a federal suffrage amendment after 1912, especially the efforts of Alice Paul and the National Woman's party. It concludes with a look at women's participation in the election of 1920, following passage of the Nineteenth Amendment, and it attempts to explain why women did not have greater political impact early in the post–suffrage era.

Chapter 1

The Colonial and Revolutionary Periods

As had been the pattern in Europe over the centuries, women in early America were not supposed to play any political role in society. Following the ideas and values brought here from the Old World, colonial leaders agreed that women's primary place was in the home, centered around traditional activities such as housework, cooking, cleaning, and childrearing. As one New Englander put it: women should "keep at home, educating of her children, keeping and improving what is got by the industry of the man."[1] In addition to taking care of the household, it was conceded, women could participate in some phases of the religious life of the community. But a sharp distinction was drawn between religion and politics. When the question arose in early Massachusetts about possibly allowing all church members a political voice regardless of their other status, Puritan minister John Cotton argued that only independent adult men had the necessary qualifications to act responsibly in the political sphere. "Women and Servants," he said, are not reckoned "capable of voting in the choice of Magistrates, ... though they may be and are, church members."[2] Cotton and others felt that women might exercise some decision-making authority within the family, but in society at large men alone could be rulers.

To be sure, not all men in early America had access to the political realm. As noted in Reverend Cotton's remarks, bound servants (primarily male) were to be excluded. Moreover, religious dissenters, white men without property, and, of course, black slaves were usually barred from any form of political participation. Members of these groups, along with women, had been traditionally looked upon as lacking the independence and personal qualities deemed essential for becoming a voter or officeholder. Yet women were clearly a special case, which is perhaps why it eventually took longer for them to legally obtain political rights. Perhaps, too, it explains why in colonial times few theorists even considered the possibility of women having any kind of political role.

In the second half of the eighteenth century, certain writers elaborated further as to why women did not belong in the political arena. A leading advice book of the time, *The Polite Lady*, published in England but widely read in America, stated that women's natural abilities were "not equal to such an arduous task" as politics. Female education, as presently conducted, said the author, was "too slight and superficial" to permit women to be "competent judges" of such matters. "I have always thought it as ridiculous for a woman to put herself in a passion about political disputes, as it would be for a man to spend his time haranguing upon the colour of a silk or the water of a diamond."[3] Just before the colonists declared their independence, Massachusetts lawyer and emerging statesman John Adams reiterated some of these views. Like the previous writer, Adams did not claim that women lacked any intellectual capacity. Rather, he believed that they were unsuited both by temperament and training for such a worldly pursuit as politics. "Their delicacy," Adams insisted, "renders them unfit for practice and experience in the great business of life, and hardly enterprises of war, as well as the arduous cares of state. Besides, their attention is so much engaged with the necessary nurture of their children, that nature has made them fittest for domestic cares."[4]

LEGAL STATUS AND POLITICAL BEHAVIOR

Laws excluding women from political rights reflected these attitudes, though not all legislators in early America saw legal disenfranchisement as essential. In fact, the idea of suffrage being for men only was so taken for granted that just one colony, Virginia, ever enacted a statute that specifically banned women from voting. A number of others—South Carolina, Georgia, and Delaware—did have laws stipulating that electors must be male, while the pronoun "he" appeared in the statute books of some of the remaining colonies. Furthermore, the term *freeman*, which was sometimes used to designate voters in New England and elsewhere, can be interpreted as a prohibition against females taking part. Nevertheless, scattered evidence indicates that not all women were denied use of the ballot in colonial times. Because most English settlers regarded property ownership as the main requirement for political participation, the authorities in some locales seem to have permitted widows possessing a substantial amount of property to go to the polls. Surviving records from a number of New England towns attest to this. Also, an item in the *New York Gazette* in June 1737, describing a recent Queens County election, noted that "two old Widdows [attended] and were admitted to vote."[5] Yet even where eligible not too many women availed themselves of the privilege of voting since it was not a practice members of the female sex customarily engaged in.

In addition to a few women voting, a small number took part in certain other kinds of political activity, especially in the seventeenth century when the colonies were still in their infancy. Perhaps the most famous incident involved Margaret Brent, an Englishwoman of considerable stature, who came to Maryland in 1648 as the executrix for the estate of deceased governor and proprietary representative Leonard Calvert. Brent, as Calvert's attorney, requested permission to speak and vote in the Maryland legislature. However, the new governor denied her wish, questioning her fitness to act in that capacity, causing Brent to protest against all measures undertaken by the existing Assembly. Six years later, another "high-born" woman, Lady Deborah Moody, who resided in Gravesend, Long Island, was personally chosen by the Dutch governor of New Netherlands, Peter Stuyvesant, to participate in the nomination of her town's officers. Moreover, in Rhode Island, the widows of well-to-do proprietors occasionally gave their consent to local civil proceedings, which can be regarded as an exercise of the political rights of landholders, even if these women could not vote in regular elections.[6]

During the half-century before the American Revolution, as the provincial political system developed further, at least a handful of women are known to have taken an open part in election campaigns. In a Georgia assembly contest in 1768, Mrs. Heriot Cooke and Miss Elizabeth Mossman drove around in a carriage soliciting votes for their favorite candidate, Sir Patrick Houstoun. They warned of dire consequences, including an increase in taxes, if Houstoun failed to win a seat in the legislature. Earlier, on two separate occasions in Lancaster County, Pennsylvania, female vote-getters made their presence felt. In the fall of 1732, Sara Galbraith of Donegal traveled all over the countryside on horseback seeking support for her husband Andrew, who stood for a legislative post. Ten years later, Susannah Wright campaigned for the Proprietary interests against the entrenched Quaker party, but was sharply criticized for her behavior in words reminiscent of later attacks on female politicians. "Could any one believe that Susy cou'd act so unbecoming and unfemale a part," declared a member of the opposition, "as to be employ'd in copying such infamous stuff [campaign broadsides] and to take her stand as she did at Lancas[te]r in an Upper Room in a publick House and to have a Ladder erected to the window and there distribute Lies and Tickets all day of the election?"[7]

WOMEN IN THE PATRIOT CAUSE

These few examples of female participation notwithstanding, the foregoing criticism reflects the fact that women were not seen as having a legitimate place in the political community. The passage of time had brought much progress to the colonies but none concerning any institutionalized political role for women. That women should have no business dealing with matters of state was an attitude maintained not only by notable men in America but also among the great minds of the late eighteenth-century European Enlightenment. Outside of the French philosopher Condorcet, no intellectual of the period seriously believed that women belonged in the public sphere. However, the American Revolution would force at least some rethinking of women's connection to the political realm here in the New World. Although no formal context existed for women entering the civil polity, they would in many ways become attached to the movement seeking political independence from England. As historian Linda Kerber has noted, women's services became highly sought after either for the army or on the home front. As a result, women were challenged to commit themselves politically and then justify their allegiance. Soon the age-old question was raised: could a woman be a patriot, an essentially political person, and, if so, what form would it take? The question, as Kerber points out, never achieved full resolution. But certainly many women, at least for a time, went beyond their traditional roles and began engaging in some kinds of public activity.[8]

From the early stages of the protest against the political and economic restrictions of the mother country, the male leadership recognized that women had a significant part to play in the resistance. In 1769 Christopher Gadsden, a prominent spokesman for the Patriot cause in South Carolina, warned husbands of the necessity of persuading "our wives to give us their assistance, without which 'tis impossible to succeed." As household managers, he and others asserted, women were as essential to the success of the economic boycotts against Britain as the men. During this time, men had in many communities created groups known as the Sons of Liberty for the purpose of promoting anti-British measures. Not long afterward, women were encouraged to form organizations called the Daughters of

Liberty with the same goal in mind. While women did not march in the streets or tar and feather uncooperative British officials, they did attempt to stop local merchants from hoarding scarce commodities and to control what could be sold. Indeed, they became deeply involved in the boycott process, helping to limit the import of British manufactures and undertaking the production of their own goods.[9]

After wearing homespun became a major symbol of the American cause, women in many locales got together for "spinning meetings" where they could enlarge the supply of home-produced materials. Although these meetings, as historian Laurel Thatcher Ulrich has recently shown, were not always meant to be self-conscious political demonstrations and in some cases had a religious purpose, a number of them clearly aimed at promoting Patriot spirit and unity.[10] The *Providence Gazette*, for example, told of a neighborhood gathering in the late 1760s, where "eighteen daughters of liberty, young ladies of good reputation," met to spin, to dine without the pleasure of tea, to purchase no more British manufactures, and to spurn any suitor who refused to support their position.[11] These spinning bees, held either in a person's home or at the local meetinghouse, were on the average attended by twenty or more women and might go on from morning till night. Men generally applauded these get-togethers and sometimes provided food and entertainment for the participants. One newspaper report, expressing approval of women joining in the endeavors against the British, hoped that the ladies "may vie with the men in contributing to the preservation and prosperity of their country and equally share in the honor of it."[12]

A more formal method of female political activity than spinning fabric was drawing up petitions protesting British measures and upholding the Patriot cause. Such petitions began to appear especially in response to the Tea Act (1773) and the Coercive or "Intolerable" Acts (1774), and showed that at least some women were fully aware of the political steps being taken by their menfolk. One petition widely acclaimed for its vigorous stance (though later lampooned in England) was that signed by fifty-one women from Edenton, North Carolina, in defense of the nonimportation resolves imposed by the First Continental Congress, late in 1774. It stated: "As we cannot be indifferent on any occasion that appears nearly to affect the peace and happiness of our country, and as it has been thought necessary for the public good, to enter into several particular resolves by a meeting of members deputed from the whole Province, it is a duty which we owe, not only to our near and dear relations and connections . . . but to ourselves, who are essentially interested in their welfare, to do everything as far as lies in our power, to testify our sincere adherence to the same; and we do therefore accordingly subscribe this paper, as a witness of our fixed intention and solemn determination to do so."[13]

Petitioning by women would continue throughout the American Revolution. However, most petitions put forth during the war tended to be individual acts, especially appeals to local governing bodies by women who had been left destitute by the upheaval. They frequently contained requests for financial aid or help in rejoining their family. Rarely were such statements the expressions of organized groups, nor could they be termed political. But other wartime behavior by women can be seen in the political guise.[14]

During the war, women engaged in many kinds of patriotic activity, some of which had clear political overtones, such as being spies and messengers, amassing provisions, or assisting military units in the field. Yet perhaps the most concerted action of a political nature was that undertaken by a group of local Philadelphia women to raise money for General Washington's soldiers. Headed by Esther DeBerdt Reed, the wife of Pennsylvania chief executive Joseph Reed, and Sarah Franklin Bache, the daughter of Benjamin Franklin, the "ladies" of Philadelphia went about the city collecting funds for the cause. Ultimately, they accumulated 300,000 paper dollars (worth perhaps $30,000). Although Mrs. Reed wanted to donate the money directly to the troops in the field, Washington convinced her that a fair allocation might be difficult to achieve. As an alternative, it was decided that the money be used to buy linen, and 2,200 shirts were made and distributed to the men in arms. The publicity stemming from this episode encouraged women in other locales to launch similar schemes to benefit the army, though none was nearly as successful. Interestingly, the attempts to justify women's participation in such quasi-political projects would be similar to the justification for women's benevolent activities in the postwar era. There was praise for women's strength of purpose and their willingness to sacrifice. But ultimately women were seen as different from men: patriotic contributors, though unsuited for a direct political role.[15]

The major political documents of the period confirm this point. The Declaration of Independence (1776) espoused no theory of women's rights, saying only that "all men are created equal," without defining exactly what this meant. The new state constitutions, enacted a short time later, generally excluded women from exercising any political power, often in a more specific manner than before. There was one exception: the state of New Jersey. Either by design or by chance, the framers of its constitution wrote that "all inhabitants of this Colony, of full age, who are worth fifty pounds," and have been residents for twelve months, "shall be entitled to vote," and this was interpreted to include unmarried women otherwise qualified. Although not too many of those eligible took advantage of the opportunity at first, a number of single or widowed New Jersey women eventually went to the polls and cast ballots. But this turn of events did not lead to similar happenings elsewhere. Most other states, beginning with New York in 1777, had made sure that women could not vote by using the word "male" to describe potential electors. Actually, in no case did the rights of women become a public issue; their exclusion was simply taken for granted.[16]

The reasons for excluding women from the political process were not usually spelled out in print. Nevertheless, the statement of Theophilus Parsons of Massachusetts in a widely read tract known as the *Essex Result* (1778) probably well expressed the prevailing male view. In words resembling those of John Adams cited previously, he wrote, "Women what age soever they are of, are . . . considered as not having a sufficient acquired discretion; not from a deficiency in their mental powers, but from a natural tendency and delicacy of their minds, their retired mode of life, and various domestic duties. These concurring, prevent that promiscuous intercourse with the world, which is necessary to qualify them for electors."[17] While Parsons declared that women should not vote because they were unworldly, Thomas Jefferson, in a letter discussing the question of representation, later argued that women should be barred from all political activity in order to prevent them from becoming worldly. This would preserve their morals, which, he said, would become endangered if they mixed "promiscuously in the public meetings of men."[18] In these comments and others like them, patriotic contributions to the war effort were ignored and long-standing ideas about women's morals and supposed "domestic" nature were considered paramount.

EMERGING WOMEN POLITICIANS

Although the above statements probably embodied the viewpoint of most men, it is clear that not all women readily consented to being barred from political life. Hannah Lee Corbin, sister of the famous Virginian Richard Henry Lee, for one, objected to this treatment. In a strongly worded letter to her brother in 1777, she urged him to support suffrage rights at least for property-holding widows. She claimed that since such women paid taxes it was unfair to impose a system of taxation without representation upon them.[19] Meanwhile, there is evidence to show that quite a few women had a high level of political awareness, despite their limited "intercourse with the world." For example, Eliza Wilkinson, a well-to-do South Carolinian, describing a meeting with her lady friends in 1779, directly challenged the idea that women lived in a state of complete ignorance. "Never were [there] greater politicians than the several knots of ladies, who met together. All trifling discourse of fashions and such low little chat was thrown by, and we commenced perfect statesmen. Indeed, I don't know but if we had taken a little pains, we should have been qualified for prime ministers, so well could we discuss several important matters in hand." In reflecting on the restraints all women of the time had to accept, Wilkinson complained that the "Lords of the Creation," would not "even allow us the liberty of thought, and that is all I want."[20]

Among northern women, two of the most well versed in politics were Sarah (Sally) Livingston Jay and Catherine (Kitty) Livingston, daughters of New Jersey governor William Livingston and both married to politically active men. Sally Jay, the wife of diplomat John Jay of New York, accompanied her husband during the war on his important foreign mission to Spain. Her letters back home were consistently filled with political subjects, although sometimes she felt the need to apologize for having "transgress'd the line that I proposed to observe in my correspondence by dipping into politicks, but my country and my friends possess so entirely my thoughts that you must not wonder if my pen runs beyond the dictates of prudence." Kitty Livingston's letters were even more heavily political than those of her sister. All through the 1780s, she corresponded with major congressional figures like Gouverneur Morris and her brother-in-law John Jay, offering comments on national affairs, especially regarding the actions of Congress. On one occasion, Kitty's brother, Henry Brockholst Livingston, remarked to her: "I know your bent for Politics, and how little you value a Letter in which a few pages are not taken up with news."[21]

One of the most prominent "female politicians" of the time was Mercy Otis Warren of Massachusetts. Like many other women concerned with public issues, Warren grew up in a political family. Her father James Otis, Sr., had long been active in high-level provincial politics; her brother James Otis, Jr., had been an outspoken critic of British rule, and her husband James Warren was a leading member of the Massachusetts legislature. Mrs. Warren would write a number of pamphlets, poems, and plays in support of the Patriot movement. One of her plays, *The Adulateur* (1772), involved a mythical kingdom named Servia, where the good subjects possessed with a love of liberty were being enslaved by a tyrannical ruler. Warren took some pride in women's contribution to the colonial resistance. "Be it known unto Britain even American daughters are politicians and patriots, and will aid the good work with their feeble efforts."[22] Although she was well aware that politics remained "a subject . . . much out of the road of female attention," she quietly defended the right of women to express their opinions. During the war period, she often corresponded with like-minded individuals such as Abigail Adams regarding the latest developments, and afterward wrote a highly partisan three-volume history of the American Revolution.[23]

Equally desirous of speaking out politically (albeit in private correspondence) was Abigail Adams, the wife of John Adams. All through the pre-Revolutionary years, Abigail had ready comments on the imperial conflict and very much favored separation from the mother country. When her husband John was a delegate to the Continental Congress in Philadelphia and beginning to formulate a new system of government, she even confided to him about what she considered a vital domestic matter—the rights of women. On the eve of American independence, Abigail wrote: "By the way in the new Code of Laws which I suppose it will be necessary for you to make I desire you would Remember the Ladies, and be more favourable to them than your ancestors. Do not put such unlimited power into the hands of the Husbands. Remember all Men would be tyrants if they could."[24] Abigail was not a modern feminist and had no wish to alter the traditional relationship between man and woman, but she obviously did want some limitation placed on the use of male power within the family. John seemed more amused than angry at the outburst but made no effort to follow through on Abigail's request. Neither did any of his congressional colleagues take up the subject.

Although John Adams had no wish to change the legal status of women or grant them voting rights, he did believe that they could hold political opinions and comment on important issues in a family setting. So frequent were his discussions with his wife on such matters that at one point Abigail declared: "What a politician you have made me."[25] Abigail Adams of all the women at the time would have welcomed the chance to use the ballot had it been given to members of her sex. On election day in 1780, she demonstrated her desire to be part of the political process by assisting at the local polling place, preparing tickets. "If I cannot be a voter upon this occasion," she said, "I will be a writer of votes. I can do some thing in that way."[26] Several years afterward, Abigail commented on the existence of woman suffrage in New Jersey, saying that "if our state constitution had been equally liberal . . . and admitted the female to a vote, I should certainly have exercised it."[27] Later, during her husband's presidency, she openly handled some of his political correspondence, even writing to Elbridge Gerry, emissary to France, amid the controversial XYZ affair in 1797. She also carried on an extensive exchange of letters with such luminaries as Thomas Jefferson after her husband left the White House.

Yet for all her interest in politics and her observance of male blunders in leadership roles, Mrs. Adams had no wish to see the new nation ruled by women. Shortly after becoming first lady of the land, she exclaimed: "Government of States and kingdoms, tho' God knows how badly enough managed, I am willing should be solely administered by the lords of creation. I should only contend for Domestic government, and think that best administered by the female."[28]

The willingness to discuss civic matters only in private settings and to leave governing entirely to men were attitudes held not just by Abigail Adams but by most politically observant women of the Revolutionary era. Why such women did not wish to go further in politics and demand an equal voice can largely be explained by the fact that women's traditional confinement to the household role was too strong to be permanently altered by the short-term experiences of the American Revolution. Their training had always been for the domestic sphere and not for the world outside. While women were capable of understanding the dynamics of the political process and in recommending courses of action, they themselves had never spent any time on the public stage and rarely thought about ascending to that level. As historian Joan Hoff-Wilson has written: "Opportunities open to women earlier in the eighteenth century were too limited to allow them to make the transition in attitude necessary to insure high-status performance in the newly emerging nation."[29] Perhaps, too, women of the time may have realized that their presence would not have been welcome if they actively sought out a greater political role in these years.

WOMEN'S POST-REVOLUTIONARY POLITICS

In any case, most post-Revolutionary era women were not necessarily unhappy remaining outside the traditionally male political sphere. In fact, many of those touched by the patriotic fervor of the Revolution, and wishing to contribute to the well-being of the new nation, found compensation in the increasingly popular idea of "Republican motherhood." Women within this mode could take pride in their domestic achievements, especially the rearing and educating of their children. Raising the next generation (sons in particular) to be moral and virtuous citizens, possibly future leaders of state, was claimed to be a patriotic endeavor ranking with almost anything that men could accomplish. To be a successful Republican mother, women were encouraged to obtain some education and an awareness of the nation's civic culture. And they could use their abilities even beyond the household at times, performing charitable work and other types of community service. It is probable that most women of the time thought such activities more fitting than ventures into partisan politics.[30]

Yet a woman's acceptance of the concept of "Republican motherhood" did not necessarily preclude an interest in state or national politics. Indeed, some women continued their close observation of political events in the immediate postwar period. They did this by reading newspapers and communicating regularly with friends and relatives on the subject. It would appear that quite a few women were aware of the high-level meetings going on in Philadelphia in the late spring and summer of 1787 that resulted in the creation of the new federal Constitution. A writer in the *Pennsylvania Gazette* that June evidently thought so as he urged "American ladies . . . to interest themselves in the success of the measures that are now pursuing by the Federal convention for the happiness of America. . . . It is in their power," he said, "by their influence over their husbands, brothers and sons, to draw them" toward a stronger central authority, and away "from those dreams of liberty under a simple democratical form of government, which are so unfriendly to that order and decency, of which nature has made them such amiable examples."[31] Whether any women responded to this plea and, if so, what form it took is unknown. We also have little evidence of women's reaction to the Constitution as eventually drafted, except for a sharply critical anti-Federalist pamphlet by Mercy Otis Warren. Interestingly, Warren did not differ from male opponents of the document in making no reference to the absence of gender in its contents.[32]

Yet if the federal Constitution ignored the female half of the population, and most politically knowledgeable women confined their political views to the private sphere, this fails to tell the whole story. As would be true over the next several decades, there were always a handful, who consciously or unconsciously defied tradition and did what society said women were not supposed to do—that is, openly participate in the political arena. One such instance was recorded in 1786 by a gentleman named Elkanah Watson on a visit to the community of Warrenton, North Carolina. On the day given to choosing representatives for the legislature, he noticed a rather large woman, who happened to be the mother of prominent Carolinian Benjamin Hawkins, actively engaged in electioneering. "I never met with a more sensible, spirited old lady," Watson observed. "She was a great politician; and I was assured, that she had more political influence, and exercised it with greater effect, than any man in her county."[33] How Mrs. Hawkins acquired her position and how she was able to gain acceptance in what was normally considered a man's domain is not easily discerned. Like many politically active women in later times, she probably benefited from the fact that she came from a politically prominent family and presumably had some education. But individual ability and character must have contributed to her success as well.

Thus, from the beginning of colonial times to the end of the Revolutionary era, women had moved from a position of being totally outside the political realm to one where they had participated in the war effort, had begun discussing current affairs, and in one state had in some cases even been admitted as voters. In terms of later developments one can, of course, argue that the amount of progress which had taken place was minimal. After all, women in general were not yet considered capable of acting responsibly in the political sphere. Nevertheless, given male attitudes at the time it might be surprising that women would have made any progress in this area whatsoever. While change would come slowly in the ensuing years, by the end of the next half-century women would begin to have more presence on the political scene.

Chapter 2

The Early National and Jacksonian Periods

Women's participation in partisan politics during the first several decades under the new federal Constitution must be divided into two parts. The initial decades—the 1790s through the 1820s—sometimes referred to as the Early National period, would see women playing a slightly larger political role than before. Occasionally they even engaged in open electioneering. For example, a Frenchman observing election day proceedings in Virginia in 1791 reported that in some towns "women go about canvassing, running from shop to shop; they beg for votes."[1] However, most of the female politicking undertaken at the time probably still occurred behind the scenes. Not until the 1830s and 1840s, in the so-called Jacksonian era, do we find women engaged in public political activity on a broad scale.

THE EARLY NATIONAL PERIOD

The period began with certain women of one state still being permitted to vote. The New Jersey Constitution of 1776 had opened the way for property-holding single women to exercise the suffrage, and they would for a time continue to do so. Indeed, in 1790, such voting was reaffirmed by statute, and the numbers at the polls gradually increased. Both parties in the state—the Federalists and the Republicans—actively campaigned for women's votes, especially around the turn of the century when the struggle between the two reached its highest levels. Yet within a few years, the Federalists, who had initially benefited the most from female voting, came to question its reliability, and the Republicans, who began to gain from the practice, were not too enthusiastic about it either. This was particularly true as women were sometimes being herded to the ballot box in a rather one-sided manner. Therefore, in 1807, following a particularly heated contest in Essex County, stained by charges of voter fraud, opponents of suffrage for women were able to bring about their disenfranchisement. Even though men were probably the main offenders regarding the behavior in question, a number of legislators claimed that women seemed the easiest persons to manipulate. Thus, they argued, in order to restore "the safety, quiet, good order and dignity of the state," their vote had to be eliminated. Shortly thereafter, without too much debate or fanfare, it was.[2]

Elsewhere, from the beginning of this era, many women maintained an interest in politics even though they had never been voters. Young women raised in political families like the future writer Catharine Sedgwick, daughter of Massachusetts congressman Theodore Sedgwick, frequently got caught up in the partisan battles between Federalists and Republicans. (Sedgwick mentions listening to her father's conversations with friends and looking upon his Jeffersonian adversaries as enemies to their country.)[3] Older women who had become accustomed to political discussion during the American Revolution appear to have carried on this tradition to a greater extent than before. The historian Mary Beth Norton claims that women were so immersed in the subject by this time, they "no longer regarded politics as falling outside their sphere" as they had in the pre-Revolutionary years.[4] Yet many men were still not quite at ease with women conversing on political topics and, at the very least, counseled them not to discuss such matters in public. Of course, some women ignored this advice, but usually any words they offered of a political nature were uttered in private. Outside New Jersey, only one woman of the time seems to have commented occasionally on politics in a public fashion, via the printed word—Judith Sargent Murray of Massachusetts. Murray, who came from a prominent New England family and was married to the leading Universalist minister, John Murray, published a number of politically related articles during the 1790s in the new *Massachusetts Magazine.* Although pro-Federalist, Murray generally bemoaned the growing party struggle and the sharp attacks made on individual character, calling instead for "peace, order, and good government."[5]

As party clashes continued into the early nineteenth century, some candidates for elective office came to realize that many women not only understood politics but also could be helpful to them in gaining voter support. Therefore, such men went out of their way to ingratiate themselves among the "ladies." For example, Daniel Tompkins, Republican governor of New York and later vice-president of the United States, it was said, had the means of securing "by his affability and amiable address, the good opinion of the female sex, who, although possessed of no vote, often exercise a powerful indirect influence."[6] But some women did more than electioneer quietly within the family. There is evidence that numerous ladies in the city of Boston attended functions held by a branch of the Washington Benevolent Society, a leading Federalist support group. In addition, a newspaper report around the time of the War of 1812 describes a local gathering of women in Vermont, which punctuated its proceedings with "the soft, clear musical discharge of a small cannon, a fit emblem of female eloquence." Among the toasts made on the occasion were "Liberty and Equality with our Companions—may we never be driven to the point where degradation and dishonor begin."[7] It is clear too that some women were beginning to make their political presence felt in Washington, D.C., the new national capital.

THE WASHINGTON SCENE

From the early 1800s, and indeed down to the present time, women with the closest connections to partisan politics have often resided in Washington, D.C. Most prominent among them at the outset was Dolley Madison, who initially handled the role of "first lady" during Thomas Jefferson's two presidential terms (1801–1809) and then continued it in the eight years of her husband James's administrations (1809–1817). Though more concerned about creating a respectable social life in the new city, Dolley did discuss political matters with people in high places, and her drawing room conversations, according to a few contemporaries, helped further James's presidential ambitions. As the time for the congressional nominating caucus approached prior to the election of 1808, Senator Mitchell of New York noted that Mr. Madison was greatly ahead of George Clinton, owing partly to the efforts of Mrs. Madison, "who aids his pretensions."[8] A year earlier, Dolley had denied to James that she was much of a politician, telling him: "I believe you would not desire your wife to be the active partisan that our neighbor is, Mrs. L, nor will there be the slightest danger, while she is conscious of her want of talent, and the diffidence in expressing those opinions, always imperfectly understood by her sex."[9] If she was not being modest and truly held those views at that moment, her later activities belie such an assertion. By the time of the War of 1812, Mrs. Madison seemed well versed in current affairs, even listening to judicial cases argued before the Supreme Court.

Louisa Adams, the wife of John Quincy Adams, was another president's spouse well versed on political subjects who acted mainly behind the scenes. Like Dolley Madison, Louisa Adams denied any close connection to politics. When a congressman once asked her opinion on a critical matter, she answered that she had "nothing to do with affairs of state." Yet Mrs. Adams, as wife of the sixth president, a man who in the White House "worked at home," obviously knew more about some consequential issues than she was willing to let on. Louisa had earlier shown political acumen in helping her husband get elected to the presidency in 1824. She had done this by visiting the wives of numerous congressmen and other officials, attending dinners and receptions, and opening her own doors to the countless political callers who came to pay their respects to Mr. Adams. Louisa Adams was aware too that in her position her personal behavior was constantly being scrutinized, especially after she became first lady of the land. "Trifling occurrences," she said, "are turned into political machinery—even my countenance was watched at the Senate during Mr. Pinkney's speech as I was afterward informed by some gentlemen." But she gradually learned to handle all public occasions in fine style. One foreigner called her "the most accomplished American lady I have seen."[10]

Another woman active on the Washington political scene in this era was Margaret Bayard Smith, the wife of a leading Republican newspaper editor. Smith's collected letters, later published under the title *The First Forty Years of Washington Society*,[11] clearly portray women in the capital as more than just social ornaments. In one communication in 1820, she mentions a friend, Caroline Breckenridge, sister of the local Episcopalian minister, who, with the Missouri statehood issue being debated, showed no interest in any socializing. "We have seen but little of Caroline B.," Mrs. Smith told a correspondent, "the Missouri question coming on she could not absent herself. She is quite enchanted with the debates and spends all her mornings at the capitol."[12] Smith, herself well versed on many subjects, was confidante of many major political figures. She carefully observed the proceedings of Congress, often attending sessions with other politically minded women to hear the orations of men like Henry Clay and Daniel Webster. Although probably referring to behind-the-scenes influence, Smith saw women exerting a greater force in politics by the start of the Jacksonian era. "Our government," she wrote in 1830, "is becoming every day more and more democratic, the rulers of the people are truly their servants and among those rulers women are gaining more than their share of power."[13]

One Washington woman in the Jacksonian era, in fact, became the central figure in a major political brouhaha: Margaret (Peggy) O'Neale Timberlake. Even the casual student of politics in this period is acquainted with the story of Peggy, the daughter of a tavern keeper, who while still married, was rumored to be involved with Andrew Jackson's future secretary of war, John Eaton. Four months after her husband's suicide, Peggy married Eaton, causing a good deal of scandal in Washington society. The episode eventually resulted in a reshuffling of Jackson's cabinet when "Old Hickory," who defended Peggy's behavior, grew angry at the wives of certain officials, including Floride Calhoun, the wife of Vice-President John C. Calhoun, for refusing to have anything to do with her. What is not so well known about Peggy are her other politically related actions, such as her seeking to influence certain federal appointments and her continuing correspondence with the new secretary of state, Jackson's close friend and ally, Martin Van Buren. Also noteworthy was her part in accompanying John Eaton throughout his senatorial campaign in Tennessee in 1832. Peggy Eaton was probably the first woman in American history to travel with her husband on an extended campaign tour, and, according to her biographer, she "thoroughly enjoyed being the center of attention" wherever they went.[14]

An equally notorious but older woman who created a stir in Washington politics around this time was Anne Newport Royall. Anne Royall, sometimes called America's first newspaperwoman, had a sharp temper and a vitriolic pen. Her attack on local religious fundamentalists once led to her being convicted under an old statute as a "common scold." (Interestingly, one of her defenders at her trial was John Eaton.) A widow who had lost her inheritance, Anne Royall at first supported herself in the 1820s by writing travel books. She then began to produce political tracts supporting the Jacksonians and in the 1832 presidential campaign started publishing a weekly paper *Paul Pry*, which aimed at exposing "all and every species of political evil."[15] Royall defended Jackson's veto of the bill rechartering the Bank of the United States and also strongly backed his efforts during the Nullification crisis with South Carolina. After 1836, Royall changed the name of her paper to *The Huntress* and modified her editorial position to a degree, moving away from a strict Democratic line. But she would continue to cover Washington politics until her eighty-fifth birthday (1854), and ferret out graft and corruption where she saw it. Public men, she said, were fair game.

More notorious nationally and far more important as a reformer and activist in American politics around this juncture was Frances "Fanny"

Wright. Born in Scotland in 1795 and very well educated for the time, Fanny Wright journeyed to this country initially in 1818 and subsequently wrote a book about what she saw as a land of hope and promise. Interested in furthering humanitarian reform, she turned to America in 1824, and, after conversations with Thomas Jefferson and James Madison, launched a highly experimental community in Tennessee with the goal of eventually emancipating slaves. Later in the decade, she moved to New York City and, with Robert Dale Owen, coedited a reformist (some would say radical) newspaper. Defying tradition, Wright started giving public lectures on political subjects—the first of her sex to do so in the United States—and soon became involved in promoting the new Working Men's party in the city of New York. Wright's speaking in public was condemned in most political circles, but her campaign efforts in 1829 helped elect several of the party's candidates to local office, men frequently referred to as "Fanny Wrightists." Although always controversial and never fully part of the political mainstream, Wright did speak favorably of Andrew Jackson when he attacked the Bank of the United States in 1832, and also urged the election of his successor Martin Van Buren during the presidential campaign of 1836. While less involved in public life after this juncture, she continued to be portrayed as a symbol of political radicalism for many years to come.[16]

WOMEN'S WIDENING POLITICAL PARTICIPATION

The 1830s was not just a time for a few celebrated women to appear on the political stage. The decade saw a significant rise in the number of women of all kinds paying attention to politics, with many eventually becoming publicly involved. Commentators like the visiting French jurist Alexis de Tocqueville, who had traveled through much of the continent, observed that now "women frequently attend public meetings and listen to political harangues."[17] There were probably several reasons for their growing interest in the subject. The broadening of democracy for males and the resurgence of party politics, while not bringing women directly into the partisan realm, did encourage a greater amount of political discussion overall. President Jackson's controversial policies and the emergence of several reform issues surely acted as catalysts as well. It can be argued, too, that the women's response was partly a reflection of their higher educational level. Many women by this point had received formal schooling, some even attending institutions for advanced learning. In certain northern towns, women had formed intellectual societies aimed at expanding the mind and increasing knowledge. What we today call "current affairs" was one of the areas emphasized. Among the topics discussed by a particular group in Austinburg, Ohio, were Andrew Jackson, the U.S. Bank, and slavery. Occasionally, such organizations adopted resolutions calling for direct action. For example, one literary society in Massachusetts resolved that "ladies ought to mingle in politics, go to Congress, etc. etc."[18]

Not surprisingly, men did not necessarily welcome women's growing interest in politics. If not always met by open male hostility, it was often received with considerable bemusement. When women expressed concern about the results of one western state's congressional contest in the fall of 1838, James Gordon Bennett, editor of the influential *New York Herald*, noted jestingly: "Even the fair ones themselves, the lovely roses of human existence—the ruby peaches of this lowly world—women, ever charming and ever interesting—particularly in the latest fashions—are asking in their small soft voice, enough to coax an angel from the sky—'do tell, have the locofocos [Democrats] carried Ohio?'" Yet even through his musings, Bennett admitted that the influence of the female intellect—female thought—and female feeling was underrated. "It should not be so," he insisted. "In all great movements of society, she exercises a powerful secret control—and so we hope she will in the coming election."[19]

At least one woman is known to have actually taken part in a congressional campaign that year, Susan McWhorter of Georgia. McWhorter, daughter of a Democratic congressman, wrote to her father's colleague James K. Polk, whom she had previously met in Washington, telling him of the plan to have her actively participate in Mr. McWhorter's reelection bid. "He says I must go with him this summer up the Country to electioneer for him. I think I can beat him among the old gentlemen at least, who are fonder of flattery than the young ones." Flattery, she adds, "is the sole secret of successful electioneering. . . . But you have been politician long enough to determine that matter yourself."[20] McWhorter's experience as a campaigner was certainly unusual, but even women in the South were increasingly in attendance at rallies and listening to speeches of the likes of James Polk.

Polk himself was no stranger to women in politics. Not only were there the wives and daughters of the congressional associates he came in contact with over the years, but his own politically savvy spouse Sarah Childress Polk. Right from the start, Sarah Polk became deeply involved in her husband's political career. An educated woman, she was conversant on most major issues of the day. Having no children, she was able to accompany James to Washington on many occasions and take part in the political festivities of the nation's capital. Back home in Tennessee, Sarah displayed her talents by handling various details of her husband's many campaigns for office. Although the times did not usually permit a wife to travel along on the hustings—Peggy Eaton had been an exception—Mrs. Polk did the next best thing. While James was making the rounds as a candidate, she constantly remained in touch through the mail, reporting on any political maneuverings she heard about. When James Polk became president of the United States in 1845, there was some doubt about his qualifications for the post, but no question of Sarah Polk's suitability as first lady.[21]

On the whole, southern women were not as likely to be involved in politics as northern women, owing to the less competitive nature of the region's political life and a more traditional attitude about what constituted proper female behavior. Perhaps typical is the remark of one southern patriarch who scolded his daughter for dabbling in politics, telling her to act as "a lady" and "be aloof" from such matters.[22] Yet some men drew a distinction between public activity and political awareness, and, while critical of public activity, found political awareness to be quite acceptable. Even such a traditionalist as John C. Calhoun, the foremost defender of the old southern system, believed that women should be politically knowledgeable and privately express their opinions. Writing to his adolescent daughter Anna Maria, who early in life began to inquire about the goings-on in Washington, he declared:

I am not one of those who think your sex ought to have nothing to do with politicks. They have as much interest in the good condition of their country as the other sex, and tho' it would be unbecoming them to take an active part in political struggles, their opinion, when enlightened, cannot fail to have a great and salutary effect. So you see, that I have no disposition to with[h]old political information from you.[23]

At first, Calhoun's correspondence with his daughter contained only brief references to current events, but as time passed he was sending her copies of his speeches and other documents to read and comment upon. Anna Maria Calhoun was not the only female South Carolinian excited by politics, for as one English visitor to Charleston later wrote, women "took a very important part" in the Nullification struggle (1832–1833), and long afterward retained "more of the enthusiastic feeling of that period than the men."[24]

SOCIAL REFORM AND ABOLITIONISM

While women may have expressed some interest in national affairs, their prime connection with the political world at this point was more likely to be in the local realm. As women were increasingly concerned with the welfare of their own communities, they often formed benevolent organizations to deal with social problems of various kinds. These groups generally provided help for the less fortunate such as visiting the sick and maintaining homes for poor widows and orphans. Although their behavior was not political in the narrow sense, women involved in these charitable works frequently came into contact with members of municipal agencies as they lobbied for changes in policy or sought to obtain funding. Even within their own organizations, women found it necessary at times to act in a political fashion, electing leaders, creating bylaws, and setting agendas. If, according to the dictates of the time, women could not openly discuss major economic and political issues—for these supposedly lay outside their sphere—they were allowed to have their say on moral issues such as prostitution and, later on, temperance and education. Indeed, women would comprise the majority of the rank and file in the local reform groups established to pursue those causes.[25]

In the northern tier of states, however, no issue did more to bring women into the larger political sphere than the abolition of slavery. By the mid-1830s, considerable numbers of women from Massachusetts to Ohio had joined female abolition societies and were playing an active part in the antislavery crusade. Seeking to pressure Congress to start placing curbs on the "peculiar institution," such societies launched a huge petition drive. Petitioning by women for political purposes was not entirely new. The tactic had been employed in America during the Revolutionary era and more recently in England in the struggle against slavery in the British Empire. Toward the end of the decade, hundreds of antislavery petitions were being circulated, and thousands of women's as well as men's signatures had been collected. The petition movement operated from three main headquarters—one in Boston, one in Philadelphia, and another in New York—with at least three women serving on the central committee for each division. Local committees were created too, containing women representatives from a vast number of towns and counties. The petition campaign, as one of the leaders pointed out, was a particularly apt means of political expression for women, whose opportunities to influence politics in other ways were extremely limited. Petitioning stimulated women's interest in the political process and taught women who were generally inexperienced in political work to be "methodical, reliable, and persevering."[26]

The abolitionist movement brought a number of women to national prominence such as Lucretia Mott in Pennsylvania and Lydia Maria Child in Massachusetts. Lucretia Coffin Mott originally came from Nantucket, Massachusetts. She grew up in a Quaker family and eventually attended a Society of Friends' school in Poughkeepsie, New York. There she subsequently became a teacher and also met her future husband James Mott, with whom she soon settled in Philadelphia. Mrs. Mott's speaking ability enabled her to become a Quaker minister, and over the years she spoke out many times on the evils of slavery. In 1833 she attended the American Antislavery Society convention organized by William Lloyd Garrison and, since women could not join the male-only AAS, helped form a female antislavery society in Philadelphia, serving as its president and guiding spirit.[27]

Lydia Maria Francis Child was born in Medford, Massachusetts. She had a good deal of formal education for the period, including a year at a woman's seminary. She was also influenced toward intellectual pursuits by her brother Convers and toward political pursuits by her husband David Child. For several years Child wrote novels and popular books for women and children, but in the early 1830s she joined the abolitionist movement and afterward devoted most of her time and energy to the cause. In 1833 she authored *An Appeal in Favor of That Class of Americans Called Africans*, which won over many converts. Later, she would edit the abolitionist weekly, the *National Antislavery Standard*.[28]

But perhaps no women would be more politically influential at this time than the Grimke sisters, who originally came from South Carolina. Sarah and Angelina Grimke had grown up in a slave-owning environment and so had directly observed the evils of black bondage. After moving north and associating themselves with abolition groups in New York and Phila-delphia, the two sisters began to do something that only the English-born "radical" Fanny Wright had dared to do in this country before—speak from a public platform on a political subject. And since they and their cause were somewhat more respectable than Fanny Wright, the impact for the future of women in politics would be much, much greater. The Grimkes' speaking out on slavery in the mid- to late 1830s would make it increas-ingly possible for other women to speak out on this and other political subjects in subsequent decades. At the outset, they appeared only before small groups of women, but then they started attracting larger groups among their sex, and after that even larger mixed audiences of men and women, sometimes numbering in the thousands.[29]

Angelina Grimke eventually addressed an open hearing of the Massachusetts state legislature in defense of female participation in the abolitionist cause. In her statement, she unhesitatingly called for the right of women to have an equal say in political matters. "Are we aliens, because we are women? Are we bereft of citizenship because we are mothers, wives, and daughters?" No, Grimke concluded, and she argued that women were active in the antislavery cause "not only because it is moral and religious, but because it is political, inasmuch as we are citizens of this republic, and as such, our honor, happiness, and well being, are bound up in its politics, government and laws."[30] Though attempting to help the slave, the Grimke sisters maintained they had no wish to become involved in traditional party politics. In fact, they always hoped men as well as women would seek to alter society through moral suasion, without a "descent" to electoral goals.[31] But ultimately some of their reform-minded successors felt that a significant change could only come about through partisan political activities.

The undertakings of the Grimke sisters and some of their allies in the abolition movement brought forth a storm of male criticism. While many men had always approved of women engaging in acts of Christian benevolence "and in all such associated effort as becomes the modesty of her sex," the idea of their taking part in petition drives, speaking out in public, and writing articles for the press was seen as going too far. As the Congregational ministers of Massachusetts had stated earlier in their "Pastoral Letter," "when [woman] assumes the place and tone of man as a public reformer . . . we put ourselves in self-defence against her; she yields the power which God has given her for protection, and her character becomes unnatural."[32] But, Sarah Grimke refused to accept the implications of this argument. In a series of published articles, she denied that women must remain in a restrictive role based on scriptural statements made thousands of years earlier. Defending her own behavior and that of like-minded members of her sex, Grimke claimed that "whatsoever is morally right for a man to do, it is morally right for a woman to do."[33]

While some men even among the abolitionists would have trouble reconciling the expanded political role that women were playing, one who rose in their defense was John Quincy Adams, former president of the United States and from 1830 until his death in 1848 a congressman from Massachusetts. Adams, who had become chief spokesman for the antislavery movement in Congress and who had grown up in a household with a politically informed mother, saw no reason why women should not be petitioning against slavery. Why, he asked, should women be discredited for taking on a political cause? Adams pointed out that they had always played some part in political affairs—from biblical women like Miriam, Deborah, and Esther to Renaissance monarchs such as Isabella of Spain. Women, he said, had demonstrated their patriotism during the American Revolution, and now female abolitionists were doing the same in their generation. Adams admitted that women had a duty to oversee household matters, but why, he wished to know, should they be limited to that domain. "I say that the correct principle is, that women are not only justified, but exhibit the most exalted virtue when they do depart from the domestic circle, and enter on the concerns of their country, of humanity, and of their God . . . when it is done from purity of motive, by appropriate means, and towards a virtuous purpose."[34]

Adams, in defending female abolitionists, claimed they were not politicians in the same manner that men were. Indeed, most women in the movement agreed, and echoed the views of the Grimkes, insisting that they had no desire to share the political stage with males or engage in partisan politics. "We are aware," one of them insisted, "that scenes of party and political strife are not the field to which a kind Providence has assigned us." Another declared: "It is not ours to fill the offices of government, or to . . . enact or enforce the laws of the land."[35] Yet as the historian Gerda Lerner has written about the effects of female abolitionist activity: "By involving large numbers of volunteers in practical political work on a grass roots level, it aroused their interest in political action. The next step was to question political candidates on their views regarding slavery, an innovation which soon became a standard method of exercising pressure on candidates and officeholders."[36] Not long afterward, some of these women were aiding in the electoral campaigns of antislavery spokesmen in their bids for Congress and other offices. Commenting on women's participation in one such contest in New England in 1841, the *National Antislavery Standard* reported: "We have seen her invited to take part in the getting up of political machinery, to influence elections. We have listened to her eulogies and poems in behalf of the people's candidates."[37] Abolitionism had indeed thrust women far deeper into politics than had been the case at any previous point of time.

PARTISAN ACTIVITY IN THE 1840s

While the abolitionist movement provided one kind of backdrop for women's entrance into the political arena, the presidential election of 1840 and subsequent party battles would provide another. In contrast to the antislavery crusade, where women quickly played a central role as organizers of petition drives and even as speakers, their open participation in the realm of partisan politics would start at a more peripheral level, far from the decision-making apparatus. Yet, in terms of numbers, female involvement in pre-election events would be much greater than at abolitionist meetings, and as the years passed the quality of women's contribution in the partisan sphere would rise too.

Women, of course, had already begun to attend campaign events in the 1830s—"listening to political harangues," as de Tocqueville described it. But starting in 1840 their participation would be much greater, owing to the unprecedented level of politicking engaged in by the emerging Whig party. The 1840 presidential contest would be seen as a watershed election in American history, particularly in terms of introducing many new vote-getting techniques. The so-called log cabin and hard cider campaign, initiated by the Whigs that year, was the first to employ huge amounts of hoopla—brass bands, slogans and songs, buttons and similar paraphernalia—and the first to appeal to the widest possible audience. To assure heavy attendance at Whig-sponsored gatherings held to promote their White House nominee "Old Tippecanoe" William Henry Harrison, party leaders sought to get women involved, encouraging them to march in parades, organize picnics, and cheer at rallies. The response far surpassed their expectations, as large numbers of female enthusiasts joined the festivities. For example, at a convention honoring Harrison in Dayton, Ohio, a Whig official counted more than 10,000 women waving "white handkerchiefs" when the Old Hero appeared. At a major party outing in Nashville, Tennessee, "more than a thousand bright eyes" greeted the revered speaker Henry Clay.[38] Especially in the mid-Atlantic and southern border states where political rivalry had always been strong, women's presence at partisan events had become a regular feature by the late stages of the contest. Indeed, one journalist claimed it was hard to find a newspaper account of a political assemblage which did not mention "that is was cheered by the approving smiles of the fair."[39]

Admittedly, most women who took part in the Whig campaign did so in an ornamental fashion—simply appearing as one of the crowd at a rally or parade. Nevertheless, some of them contributed in a more individual and substantial way, sewing party banners and doing other helpful tasks. Amelia Bloomer, later a leading suffragist and reformer, sat in on political meetings and also assisted in the preparation of badges and mottoes to be used by Whig marchers in her hometown of Seneca Falls, New York.[40] At least one woman, a midwesterner by the name of Lucy Kenney, wrote a campaign tract in behalf of candidate Harrison, and a few women even delivered partisan speeches for the cause. In Vandalia, Illinois, Miss Jane Field gave a rousing address to the county delegates headed to the state party convention regarding the need to drive the "Tarquins" (i.e., locofoco Democrats) from all places of power.[41] In addition, many women attended public lectures created especially for them by such nationally renowned figures as Daniel Webster, with the idea that they might subsequently influence the votes of male family members. Whig leaders were convinced that most women understood what was at stake in the election—the need to oust the corrupt administration of Andrew Jackson's handpicked successor Martin Van Buren—and were on their side. As one pro-Whig editor from Ohio remarked, if women possessed the franchise, they would "sweep Locofocoism from this country in short order," and another newspaperman declared that "women are the heart and soul of these movements." "From Maine to New Orleans," it was proclaimed, "our mothers, sisters, and daughters are now, as in the days of the Revolution, all Whig."[42]

On the Democratic side, some attempt was made to match the Whig effort in building popular support and reaching out to women. Francis Blair, longtime Jacksonian and editor of the party's leading newspaper, the *Washington Globe*, a man whose own wife and daughter were politically knowledgeable, encouraged women at least to act in a private capacity in behalf of the party cause. Long before the election, Blair had urged his female readers to "employ for what they may consider their own and the country's interests, all the persuasive influence not only of fact and argument . . . but the persuasion of every sentiment and sympathy which the most intimate of family ties beget" to affect the outcome.[43] But compared to the Whig exertions not too much was done to mobilize women to attend political events. In fact, certain Democratic spokesmen decried the new practice of "dragging women into politics," claiming that this would lead to their ruination. As a writer in the *North Carolina Standard* put it: "For the vulgar strife of politics, her sensibilities are too refined, and for its fierce contention, her nerves are too delicate. Her weakness is her surest protection, and her softness is her best ornament. We have been pained therefore, during the pending struggle for the Presidency, which has been distinguished for its bitterness, to see our fair countrywomen unsex themselves, and stepping across the threshold to mingle in the fight."[44]

Whether the above statement was merely partisan rhetoric or whether, like the earlier "Pastoral Letter," it truly reflected the belief that those turning themselves into "female politicians" would become unsexed, countless men continued to voice such views over the next eighty years. Their words grew ever more frequent once women started asking for the vote in 1848. Yet while most of those in power would have agreed that women should not possess suffrage rights, less of a consensus existed on whether they should be kept out of politics altogether. If some men wanted to bar women from all aspects of political life, many others seemed to accept and even encourage their participation as long as it stayed on a subordinate plane. The very fact that women in many places became a permanent fixture in campaigns after 1840 indicates that the men in charge were not averse to their presence. It also implies that for these politicians gaining the spoils of office was much more important than the abstract principle of keeping women within their "sphere." It is likely that most party leaders never considered the whole subject very seriously and did not foresee that employing women in auxiliary positions would lead to anything beyond that.

One man who certainly appreciated women's presence at various campaign events was Whig leader Henry Clay of Kentucky, especially when he ran for the presidency in 1844. Although perhaps not in favor of full political equality for women, Clay even more than John C. Calhoun or John Quincy Adams thought women deserved to occupy a place in the political realm. Admired by the ladies of the period more than any of his contemporaries—some say he would have easily been elected to the White House if female opinion had been taken into consideration—Clay often responded positively to invitations by groups of women to speak in their town or city. "I hope," he once said, "the day will never come when American ladies will be indifferent to the fate and fortunes of our common country, nor fail on rare and critical occasions, to demonstrate their patriotic solicitude, in a manner suitable to the delicacy and dignity of their sex."[45] Ad hoc female clubs created to promote Clay's candidacy during the election of 1844—the first of their kind anywhere—were far more numerous than those formed for his rival James Polk, even in Polk's home state of Tennessee.

In fact, throughout the decade of the 1840s, the Whigs proved more successful in enlisting women's support than the Democrats. Partly this reflected a greater willingness to take a moral stance on issues and to employ feminine symbols. Furthermore, the Whigs had stronger ties among families of the middle and upper classes, whose female members were more likely to have the time and inclination to participate in politics. In encouraging them to make a few appearances during campaigns, Whig leaders had no wish to make women give up their traditional roles and become full-time politicians. In fact, as Mary P. Ryan has pointed out, the Whigs were appealing to "the same constituency that, during the same period, spawned a domestic ideology celebrating both feminine and private virtue. When the Whigs sang 'Home Sweet Home,' they honored the wives, daughters, and mothers . . . who were recent subscribers to the cult of domesticity."[46] The Democrats, on the other hand, when asking for female assistance, did not place much emphasis on moral positions or on feminine symbolism. Indeed, they made far fewer overtures to women than their opponents. The fact that the Democrats' strongest constituencies lay among southerners and among urban immigrants, whose menfolk showed less desire for reform or in seeing women politicized, perhaps explains their side's smaller interest.

While numerous women helped out the major parties, in terms of the ratio between male and female participants, perhaps a greater percentage of the women would be active on behalf of the new, short-lived Native American party. Formed in the early 1840s, chiefly in the seaboard states from Massachusetts to Maryland, the Nativists' main goal was to limit the rapidly expanding foreign (heavily Catholic) immigration and the political influence of foreigners already in the United States. Although the party's regular organization in each state was entirely male, party auxiliaries with names such as the Female Native American Association, Native American Benevolent Association, or American Republican Benevolent Association soon sprang up in the large cities of the mid-Atlantic states such as Philadelphia and New York, and gradually spread elsewhere. Many non-partisan female nativist societies were created as well. Membership in such groups included not only housewives but also working women, who, along with working men, disliked the influx of cheap European labor into the country. Like women attached to the mainstream parties, most of those connected to the Native American party cheered at parades and attended mass meetings. A few, however, served the movement as propagandists, contributing articles and letters to the press. One such woman, Harriet Probasco of Pennsylvania, briefly published a partisan newspaper during the campaign of 1844 and helped mobilize the female forces of her state for the Nativist cause.[47]

It is perhaps something of a paradox to find the highest proportion of female participants among the Nativists, the most conservative political organization of the period. Indeed, its policymakers recognized the dilemma of encouraging women to become politically active, while at the same time believing that they belonged in the domestic sphere. However, given their opinion that foreign immigrants would destroy the existing Protestant American culture, Nativist leaders felt that the overriding need to save the nation required female public involvement in this instance. They defended women's part in nondomestic activities by claiming that their service constituted a patriotic, not a partisan, action. In this way, they argued, women could exert an influence on society at large without violating the bounds of propriety. The women, they insisted, were not full partners but were "coadjutors in the cause," joining in a cooperative effort to preserve the existing American way of life. The emphasis on women's patriotism here was similar to the rhetoric used in defense of Republican motherhood in the post-Revolutionary era. What was new in these pronouncements was the extension of woman's position as moral guardian of the home to an increasingly public level.[48]

While women attached to each of the parties in the 1840s won praise for their efforts, the role they played was clearly circumscribed. With few exceptions, their function consisted of hosting picnics, watching parades, or attending rallies. They had no official standing in any party organization and were unable to exert real influence. They could not make policy, run for office, or vote. Much of what women did in the partisan sphere took place far away from the centers of power. But were these women necessarily unhappy in their peripheral position? Did these women feel used and taken advantage of? Although women party workers in later periods may have harbored such feelings, there is little evidence of female discontent at this point regarding their subordinate status. Most women seem to have been happy to contribute to what they believed was a worthy cause, albeit in a limited way. They undoubtedly took pride in being included in the nation's political process and in being given the opportunity to benefit society, though some surely would have welcomed the chance to do more.

In one short-lived movement around this time, women did get to do more: the episode known as the Dorr Rebellion (1841–1842). In Rhode Island not only women but also more than half of the men had no political rights under the old colonial charter that served as the constitution. When the attempt to substitute a new "People's Constitution," giving all men the vote, was rejected by existing voters—limited to the freeholder class—opponents of the old system chose their own set of leaders, headed by Thomas Dorr. Moving quickly, they soon took control of the northwestern part of the state. The old governor then declared the Dorr party as insurrectionary and called out the state militia to resume authority. Ultimately, the Dorr Rebellion was put down and Dorr himself imprisoned. Nevertheless, the remaining members of the cause sought to keep the goal of suffrage expansion alive, and created the Dorr Liberation Society to work toward that end. In this effort women played a prominent role. As described by a recent historian of the Dorrite movement: "Women staged political rallies, organized clambakes, drafted petitions and otherwise publicized the Dorrite cause. They did this in defiance of martial law," apparently believing that countermeasures by the authorities would not be applied so severely to them. Moreover, "Dorrite women never asked that the vote be extended to them, a fact which enforced their deradicalizing role in the Rhode Island struggle."[49]

Another phase of women's political activity at this juncture was associated with the less than desirable labor conditions at the textile mills in Lowell, Massachusetts. In these years the city of Lowell had become a major center for textile production, with native-born young women performing the bulk of the factory work. Women had entered the mills to help supplement family income or to provide money for their own dowries. The wages and working conditions had not been bad at first, but the owners' attempt to offset losses during the economic downturn of the late 1830s brought lower pay and a speed-up of the machines. Women began to protest against these changes through strikes and petitions. They also formed the Lowell Factory Ladies Reform Association (LFLRA) and appealed to the legislature to provide relief through a maximum ten-hour workday. In 1845 workers' petitions numbered over 1,150, three-fourths of the signatures coming from women. While the legislature appointed an investigating committee and permitted women to testify before it, the committee report recommended no action be taken. In response, the LFLRA sought to discredit the report and to defeat at the polls its prime author, state representative William Schouler, at the next election. Indeed, its efforts were successful, and afterward the association thanked the voters "for consigning . . . Schouler to the obscurity he so justly deserves."[50] The association continued to exist in the years to come, but subsequent protest action in Lowell became increasingly male dominated as petition campaigns "gave way to ward political work," according to labor historian Thomas Dublin.[51]

DECLINE OF PARTISAN ACTIVITIES

Just as women's partisan activity declined in Lowell, it is probable that by the late 1840s it was beginning to level off elsewhere, at least temporarily. The number of newspaper stories mentioning women's attendance at political events fell considerably, though this may partly mean their appearance was becoming less of a novelty. It may also reflect the fact that there were fewer campaign demonstrations of any kind after the heated presidential contest of 1844, when the "dark horse" Democrat James K. Polk narrowly defeated the famous Whig leader Henry Clay. The national election of 1848, though featuring a new reform party, the Free Soilers, which attracted some female adherents, did not produce as much excitement as the previous two races. None of the three main presidential contestants—Zachary Taylor (Whig), Lewis Cass (Democrat), or Martin Van Buren (Free Soil)—stimulated much public enthusiasm among either gender. In addition, the beginning of the women's rights movement sparked by the Seneca Falls Convention, where several radical demands were made including equal suffrage, may have had a negative effect on female partisan activity, especially in the South. To southerners, this new crusade became closely associated with abolitionism and "Fanny Wrightism," making men reluctant to encourage women's participation in any kind of politics. It probably caused some of the women themselves to have second thoughts about engaging in behavior increasingly seen as unladylike.[52]

In any case, regardless of a temporary decline, women had come a considerable distance in the field of politics since the start of the Early National period. At that time, the extent of their partisan activity was limited to a few individuals operating primarily behind the scenes. Yet by the early 1830s women in general were starting to pay greater attention to partisan affairs and even attend party events. The rise of the abolitionist movement, as the decade progressed, brought many additional women into the world of political activity. More than anything else, the Whig campaign of 1840 marked a turning point in terms of female involvement. During that and subsequent contests women mainly watched and cheered, though they also formed partisan clubs and in a few cases made substantial contributions with their pen and voice. In addition, they took part in protests at the Lowell mills and in the Dorr Rebellion. Women were by no means at the core of all political proceedings but no longer functioned only on the periphery.

Chapter 3

The Civil War Period

As noted at the conclusion of the previous chapter, American women began to play a bigger part in partisan politics in the early 1840s followed by somewhat of a decline in the late 1840s. Nevertheless, if a decline occurred it was rather short-lived, for the 1850s would see a heavier degree of participation than before, at least in the northern states. There, interest in reform and in the expanding sectional crisis would ultimately lead many women to cooperate with men in the launching and subsequent promoting of the new Republican party. Meanwhile, in the South, the rapid decline of the Whigs as viable opponents of the Democrats would sharply reduce direct involvement in partisan electoral activities. Yet at the same time, a few southern women would take up their pens and vigorously defend their section from outside attack, and at the end of the decade many more would openly encourage the idea of secession from the Union. But prior to that juncture almost the entire wave of new female activism came from above the Mason-Dixon line.[1]

THE NEW WOMEN IN POLITICS

The growing involvement of northern women in the political process was the result of many factors, some representing trends that had begun in previous years. For one thing, the number of women in the workforce was increasing and was presumably contributing to a heightened political awareness. For another, women's educational level was gradually rising.

By midcentury, girls in most states could attend public schools, and a few were even enrolled in college. Altogether at least half the women in America could read and write. Furthermore, the proliferation of newspapers, the majority of which were highly partisan and filled with political news, gave more women as well as men a stronger sense of what was going on in politics than had been the case before. Women also continued to attend public meetings where political questions like slavery expansion were discussed. Women's reform groups dealing with issues such as temperance kept attracting members too. In addition, the women's rights movement began to publicize matters of specific concern to their sex, for example, property rights and custody of children. Although most women did not immediately jump into partisan activities, they probably did begin to take greater notice of them, and for some this set the stage for subsequent participation.[2]

Among the new women entering the political arena were many of those reformers, who in prior years had always distanced themselves from partisan politics. A major reason for this reversal in attitude was their feeling that the traditional methods of achieving reform in society such as moral suasion had not been successful. Before this time, as Lori D. Ginzberg has written, women reformers, "viewed as inherently moral, were supposed to instruct by example" and somehow transform the public soul without becoming political.[3] But their efforts under the auspices of female associations had not produced any fundamental societal change. While some reformers inevitably continued working in the old established pattern, others began to shift toward a new mode that promised better results. Over the next decade, women's involvement in purely benevolent movements would diminish and become less visible, whereas their participation in direct political action would rise and become more visible. In contrast to the past, they "increasingly framed their conception of social change in terms of electoral means and goals." The 1850s, as Ginzberg demonstrates, "witnessed a burst of legislative activity on the part of women; hundreds and thousands demanded their civil rights and joined men in appealing for laws against alcohol, for removal of politicians and judges, and for corporate charters and funds for their organizations."[4] It also saw women attending local partisan gatherings in greater numbers, even if the atmosphere was not always congenial to those of their sex. As this phenomenon grew, the women's rights' newspaper *The Lily*, using an ironic tone, proclaimed, "Yes, our ladies have mingled at political meetings with the 'low rabble' who go to the polls."[5] But this mingling was not a smooth and easy process, for male leaders mainly concentrated on mobilizing actual voters who were men. Furthermore, some traditionalists raised their voices more loudly than ever against the presence of women in partisan politics.

DEBATE OVER WOMEN IN POLITICS

Indeed, the upsurge in women's political activity in the 1850s led to a growing number of public statements condemning the emergence of so-called female politicians, and not just from men. Sarah Hale, editor of *Godey's Lady's Book*, the most influential mainstream woman's magazine of the time, insisted that women should shun political issues and the idea of joining partisan groups. These only made her sex conspicuous, said Hale. Women's sphere was not a public one, and in her view there was nothing more unlovely than a female politician. Defects in the laws, she declared, should be left to "our rulers and statesmen." Hale herself occasionally sought government aid for projects to promote patriotism or to provide help for the needy, but she apparently drew the line at this point.[6] Another woman who criticized female political behavior beyond a certain level was an anonymous contributor of articles to a San Francisco newspaper in 1856. "Nellie" praised women's support of the vigilante movement to clean up corruption and vice in that city, but warned against their straying too far from home for such purposes. In prior letters to the editor, she had disparaged women's rights advocates, and presumably she would have frowned upon women's involvement in any kind of electoral activity.[7]

One of the strongest rebukes leveled at politically active women appeared in an essay published in the partisan *Democratic Review* just prior to the presidential election of 1852. The anonymous author, undoubtedly male, was clearly upset with the way women in the previous decade, "under that wild infatuation of party enthusiasm, . . . forsook their home paths and appeared in public" in a variety of political activities.[8] Part of his anger may have stemmed from the fact that the opposition parties had benefited more than his; yet his tone implies something deeper. The author saw women politicking as an outrage of female behavior, taking on "the character of frenzy, public display, personal animosities, and unfeminine virulence." He understood the attraction of participating in campaigns compared to the "common pursuits" of the household, but, he went on, "such aberration from the sacred domestic routine cannot often be repeated without serious effects upon the delicate harmonies of the family and social structure." In a plea to menfolk not to use women for electioneering purposes, he exclaimed: "Let fathers and husbands, then, look to it how, for a transient and doubtful political triumph, they themselves let down the barriers of female decorum."[9] The long-term benefits to women themselves were questionable too, he added.

Assessing the experiences of female politicians from times past, the article's author claimed that the lives they led did not bring them much contentment. He asserted that almost without exception those individuals who had been "ambitious of political sway" like Empress Catherine of Russia and Queen Marie Antoinette of France wound up "conspicuously unhappy" and guilt ridden for all their efforts. He then went on to praise the wives of our nation's founders such as Abigail Adams and Martha Washington, who dutifully served their husbands at home and did not enter the public arena. He also extolled the virtues of Mary Washington, the mother of the first president, who devoted her best years to raising her illustrious son. Women, he believed, in line with the earlier "Republican motherhood" argument, should use whatever learning and other abilities they possessed for the good of their families and their country, but never in a partisan political manner. "We should have our women Americans, in the loftiest sense of the term; true Republicans, devoted patriots, but faithful to their own orbit, receiving and giving light in their own natural path; patriots, not politicians, angels not agitators."[10] Although most male leaders at the time probably would have agreed with this summary view, they did not always adhere to it in practice, especially where they saw they could use women to good political advantage.

As in previous years, a few prominent men publicly defended the idea of women's political participation, occasionally using an argument that would grow common in the Progressive period, that the infusion of women would have a cleansing effect on politics. One of these men was the well-known minister and abolitionist Henry Ward Beecher, brother of Harriet Beecher Stowe. In a speech at the Cooper Union in New York City at the end of the decade, Beecher declared that women, if given the opportunity, could help reform government. Clearly, government as it presently existed "needed improvement," he said, as men frequently sank to using "force, passion and fraud" in the conduct of public affairs. Concerning the charge that women would be defiled by the hurly-burly of politics, he answered that society had nothing to fear "because there wouldn't be any hurly-burly after she got in. . . . Man and woman would be a better business in politics together."[11] With regard to their involvement, Beecher did not think every woman should go as far as to become a candidate for office, but he did want those who were capable to have their share. No one had any objection to Jenny Lind's singing on the concert stage, he declared, so why not apply the same rule to some other gift. Beecher noted that Queen Victoria of England was the "proudest monarch reigning." But when it came down to "plain democratic women," the world unfortunately objected to them having much say.[12]

Regardless of the debate, many women continued to express their political concerns, though at times confessing to an uneasiness about it. One prominent California woman confided: "I find myself deeply interested in politics this season, though Sister Mattie Cole thinks it sinful of me."[13] A lady from Indiana wrote that she had become "that *unenviable character*, a *political woman*," but the gravity of the political crisis had "aroused every feeling of patriotism and justice of which my woman's heart is capable of feeling."[14] Julia Ward Howe, later author of the "Battle Hymn of the Republic" and a leading abolitionist, described her entrance onto the political stage in the 1850s in similar terms. "I deeply regretted the discords of the time, and would have had all people good friends, however diverse in political persuasion." But as this could not be, Howe said she felt constrained to enter the fray, "against the new assumptions of the slave power."[15] Men understood that while women could not vote they could influence the menfolk in their family, and several editorialists deliberately appealed to women to do so. Women themselves recognized their ability to affect what transpired on the political scene. "We *have* influence," one woman told former President Millard Fillmore.[16]

THE RISING TIDE OF SECTIONALISM

Beyond a general desire for reform, northern women's stepped-up participation in politics in these years was intimately related to the rise of sectional tensions. This started to happen following the breakdown of the Compromise of 1850, which had sought to smooth over North-South differences concerning possible expansion of slavery into the western territories acquired at the end of the Mexican War. Interestingly, one of the most controversial figures in the burgeoning sectional conflict was a woman: Harriet Beecher Stowe, the author of *Uncle Tom's Cabin* (1852). Stowe, though raised in an abolitionist family, had not been involved in the public debate over the slave issue before this time. She had written a number of stories but never any with an obvious political theme. However, her antislavery sensitivities were aroused by the passage of the strong Fugitive Slave Law, which had been a key part of the 1850 compromise legislation. (The Fugitive Slave Law required that the full authority of the federal government be placed at the service of slaveholders seeking to recapture runaway slaves.) Stowe's novel stirred northerners to see not only the horrors of slavery but the humanity of the slaves as well. It also caused them to start thinking about taking public action on the slavery issue.[17]

The publication of *Uncle Tom's Cabin* was part of a series of events in the early to mid-1850s that would lead to political realignment, one in which women would play a conspicuous role. In the winter of 1854, as Congress debated the Kansas-Nebraska bill, which threatened to open new western territories to slavery, Harriet Beecher Stowe entered the political arena more directly than through her novel, and urged other women to do the same. She published an "Appeal to the Women of the Free States," calling on each of her female readers to fully understand the impending legislation "for herself," and "feel that as mother, wife, sister, or member of society, she is bound to give her influence on the right side." Stowe then asked women to launch petition drives against the bill and to circulate antislavery tracts to help other people comprehend the situation.[18] How many women participated in such activities is not known, but whatever the number, their labors turned out to be of little avail in getting congressmen to change their vote on the measure. Nevertheless, the encounter brought more women into the political process and must have encouraged their interest in the possibility of a new political party based on antislavery principles.

RISE OF THE REPUBLICAN PARTY

Following passage of the Kansas-Nebraska Act in 1854, which repealed the Missouri Compromise and opened further the possibility of slavery spreading into the western territories, the existing political parties—Whigs and Democrats—began to experience widescale defections. Many northerners, regardless of their previous political affiliation, became attracted to the idea of a new party, one that would prevent any additional expansion of slavery in the West. Soon the Republican party was born, and considerable numbers of women, moved by its ideals, quickly volunteered to support the new organization. Indeed, the press reported that the very first Republican gathering anywhere in the country—in the town of Ripon, Wisconsin, in March 1854—was "largely attended by persons of both sexes."[19] Other notices of early Republican meetings also mention women being part of the scene. Senator John Sherman of Ohio later recalled that during the party's first year, meetings were frequently held in churches "with an audience of men, women and children present."[20] In 1855, women's rights activist Elizabeth Cady Stanton, whose husband Henry had joined the party in upstate New York, wrote to her friend and fellow reformer Susan B. Anthony, telling her that she had recently "attended all the Republican meetings" in her locale.[21]

Inspired by the Republicans' antislavery vision and the nomination of John C. Frémont as the party's standard-bearer, many more women than ever before took part in an election drive when the new organization launched its first national campaign in 1856. At a rally in Paterson, New Jersey, a reporter noted that "a large portion of the audience was composed of women." In Buffalo, New York, a correspondent observed what he felt was "a new feature in political gatherings . . . the presence of some 400 ladies" among the cheering Republican throng. At a huge parade in Indianapolis "were to be seen thousands of fair ladies, waving handkerchiefs as the procession passed." Abraham Lincoln, at one political meeting in the state of Illinois, counted more than seventy mothers with nursing babies among the crowd. Not all pro-Republican women were able to take an active part in each of the local festivities. Elizabeth Cady Stanton, for one, having six young children in her care, regretted that she often had to remain at home while her husband Henry was out campaigning for Frémont. Nonetheless, the depth of commitment was impressive. Overall, according to Indiana Republican George Julian, "No political campaign had ever been . . . cheered by such a following of orderly, intelligent, conscientious and thoroughly devoted men and women."[22]

One woman particularly enthusiastic about this contest was the writer and longtime abolitionist Lydia Maria Child. Previous runs for the presidency featuring the likes of Henry Clay and Zachary Taylor had not truly sparked her interest, but here the circumstances were different. "For the first time in my life," she said, "I am a *little* infected with *political* excitement. For the sake of suffering Kansas, and future freedom in peril, I *do* long to have Frémont elected," she wrote to a friend. In the later stages, she expressed guilt about not doing enough for the Republican cause. "My anxiety on the subject has been intense. It seemed as if my heart would burst if I couldn't *do* something to help the election." She eventually did write a story about the slavery expansion threat called "The Kansas Emigrants," which was serialized in the *New York Tribune*.[23] Even more active on the Republican side was Clarina Howard Nichols, a native Vermonter, who had recently settled in Kansas and served as a lecturer for the New England Emigrant Aid Society. Nichols spoke on more than fifty occasions during the 1856 campaign, focusing not only on the slavery issue but also on women's rights.[24] Another New England woman who went to Kansas also deserves mention: Hannah Ropes, who wrote an important tract criticizing Franklin Pierce and his Democratic administration for its mishandling of the matter of slavery in the new territories.[25]

Clearly the most influential woman in the 1856 presidential race was Jessie Benton Frémont, wife of the Republican nominee, John C. Frémont. Jessie Frémont, the well-educated daughter of former Missouri senator Thomas Hart Benton, had long been exposed to politics and took on more responsibilities than any previous candidate's spouse. According to historian Allan Nevins, Jessie played "only a slighter part in the contest than her husband."[26] Right from the beginning, she supervised his incoming campaign correspondence, deciding which letters and newspapers should reach Mr. Frémont, and in so doing protecting him from vicious opposition attacks. She also compiled material for the principal campaign biography (authored by John Bigelow) and answered reporters' questions about her husband's controversial past. A confident woman, long accustomed to backstage maneuvering in Washington, Jessie declared that she was able "to look into the political cauldron when it was boiling without losing my head."[27] So popular was the young Mrs. Frémont with the public at large that many party banners that year carried the words "John and Jessie" or "Frémont and Jessie," virtually ignoring the Republican vice-presidential candidate Jonathan Dayton of New Jersey.

Two years later, in 1858, during the famous Illinois senatorial contest, women were again conspicuous, particularly in attending the series of debates between rival candidates Abraham Lincoln and Stephen A. Douglas. A contemporary lithograph shows several Republican women on one of those occasions holding a large banner bearing the inscription: "WESTWARD THE STAR OF EMPIRE TRAILS ITS WAY; THE GIRLS LINK ON TO LINCOLN, THEIR MOTHERS WERE FOR CLAY."[28] Interestingly, both candidates' spouses were among the most politically active and knowledgeable female figures of the time. Lincoln's wife Mary Todd, from a prominent Kentucky family, had long displayed a concern for public affairs, listening attentively to the conversations of various politicians who visited her home both when she was growing up and later on during her marriage. She had many political discussions with her husband and is said to have influenced his views against slavery. Although Mary felt that the women's rights movement with its public protests was unladylike, she had no qualms about engaging in her own political activity behind the scenes. According to her recent biographer Jean Baker, Mary Lincoln "tried to encourage in her husband the conviction that he could be president, and she entertained those who might help what she considered their mutual campaign." Adele Cutts of Maryland, who in the 1850s became Douglas's second wife, was, like Mary Todd Lincoln, a woman of impeccable breeding and similarly encouraged her husband's career. Several times she accompanied him on his senatorial campaign trips, and in the capitol she often sat in the gallery during his speeches.[29]

The woman perhaps most deeply involved in the partisan activities of this era was Anna Ella Carroll of Maryland (1815–1890). The daughter of Thomas King Carroll, one-time governor of the state, the well-educated Anna Carroll early in life developed a fascination for politics. She subsequently used her political contacts to seek patronage appointments for friends and relatives, particularly her father, whose fortunes had faded following his governorship. From the experience she gained as a freelance writer, the never married Miss Carroll soon began to promote her own career as a party publicist. At first siding with the Whigs in the early 1850s, Carroll, like many other Americans of the time, became upset over the large influx of immigrants (especially Catholics) and joined the nativist movement. During the national campaign of 1856, she wrote several works in behalf of the American or Know-Nothing party, seeing it as a bulwark against the expanding power of "political Romanism" in this country. The most influential of her writings was a lengthy, passionately worded tract entitled *The Great American Battle*. Besides her many publications, Carroll carried on a prodigious correspondence with various American party officials. She was an ardent admirer of ex-President Millard Fillmore and a strong advocate of his nomination as the party's standard-bearer that year. Carroll contributed a number of pamphlets praising his candidacy, but she felt inadequately rewarded for her effort. Fillmore, though grateful for her support, became annoyed at her constant demands for personal attention and financial remuneration, and kept his distance. Over the next few years, Carroll, having become concerned about the growing sectional tensions, worked to promote a fusion of the Know-Nothings with the new Republican party. When this failed and Abraham Lincoln was elected president in 1860, Carroll, a strong unionist, finally switched to the Republican side. During the Civil War, she would write pamphlets praising the Lincoln administration, including "The War Powers and the Government" and "The Relation of Revolted Citizens to the National Government," and also used her pen to try to influence the president's wartime strategy.

Through all these political endeavors, Anna Carroll was well aware of the uniqueness of her position. In fact, in works such as *The Great*

American Battle, she apologized for her intrusion into the masculine world of politics. Carroll declared that she had "no aspirations to extend her influence or position," and had no wish to challenge the principles that placed woman "in a sphere at variance with that refined delicacy to which she is assigned by nature." Yet like the nativists a decade earlier Carroll pointed to the danger the nation was facing, and argued that she knew no rule excluding females from "the discussion of any subject which has an immediate bearing on the social, moral, and political destiny of this nation." It should be recognized, too, that "the interests and destiny of mothers and daughters are common with those of fathers and brothers," she added. In her call for a revival of morality and patriotism, Carroll claimed that God had given women the chief responsibility for leading the reformation of America. Woman's high political mission is to act as "a moral agent" to regenerate the country. "The fate of America," she concluded, was dependent on the work of "America's daughters."[30]

Most politically aware women were not as active or outspoken as Anna Carroll and probably did not see their societal role in such grandiose terms. More typical perhaps was the experience of Mary Baker Eddy, who only occasionally exercised her pen for political purposes. Later the founder of Christian Science, Mary Baker grew up in a Jacksonian Democratic home in New Hampshire and absorbed her father's political views. Although Mary personally disliked slavery and, while living in the South with her first husband George Glover, once anonymously criticized the institution, she shied away from any harsh words on the subject upon returning to the North in the 1850s. In fact, extreme abolitionism and the spreading North-South conflict truly disturbed her and made her fear for the future of the Republic. Mary was a friend of Franklin Pierce, the Democratic candidate in 1852, and published an admiring sonnet during his presidential campaign. (Pierce generally shared her desire to preserve the political status quo.) However, further on in the decade as sectional differences widened and Pierce along with his Democratic successor James Buchanan refused to take forceful action to uphold the Union, Mary began shifting her sympathies and grew openly critical of those in power. She once wrote the following lines for publication: "O! weak Buchanan, join thy country cause, and aid her champions to defend her laws."[31] By the time of the outbreak of hostilities in 1861, she was a committed Republican and supporter of the Lincoln wartime administration. Yet in the postwar years, as she became a famous religious leader, Mary Baker Eddy declined to take any open stands on issues or attach herself to any particular political party.

SOUTHERN WOMEN DEFEND THEIR SECTION

Although southern women were less likely to be publicly involved with politics than northern women, and less likely to find approval for such behavior, a few did stand up to defend the South and its institutions through published letters and essays in major magazines. Louisa McCord of South Carolina, daughter of Langdon Cheves, former head of the Second Bank of the United States, wrote several works in defense of slavery. If she offered no original theories, she did expound her views with great passion. In a caustic review of *Uncle Tom's Cabin*, McCord questioned the credibility of many episodes in the novel and, in general, claimed the work was filled with "vulgarity and falsehood." Slaves in the South, she argued, were treated in a benign manner. The institution was not "a sorrow and a wrong to live down," but on the contrary, "a Godlike dispensation, a providential caring for the weak," and a refuge for "nature's outcasts." McCord did not believe in changing the ways of free white women's lives any more than those of the slaves, and scorned the efforts of women's rights activists in the North seeking to acquire equal suffrage.[32]

Another female southerner who publicly defended the existing order in the plantation region was Julia Gardiner Tyler, wife of ex-President John Tyler. Although raised in New York, Tyler spent most of her adulthood in Virginia, especially after her husband's retirement from national politics. Like McCord, she attracted considerable attention through a long letter that appeared in the *Southern Literary Messenger* shortly after Stowe's book appeared. In her statement, Tyler praised the civilizing mission of the slave system and denounced critics who attacked it. Later on, in another public letter, Tyler defended southern women in response to the charges of a British lady that they were indifferent toward slavery and particularly the point that they lacked an awareness of anything going on outside their immediate locale. The women of the southern states, Tyler wrote, are for the most part "well educated" and "have peculiar opportunities of acquiring knowledge in regard to the public concerns of the world. Politics is almost universally the theme of conversation among men, in all their coteries and social gatherings, and the women would be stupid indeed, if they did not gather much information from this abundant source."[33]

In the fall of 1859, following John Brown's raid at Harper's Ferry, Virginia, which had sought to stir up a massive slave rebellion, another southern woman took up her pen in defense of her section. Margaretta Mason, wife of the Virginia senator who had framed the Fugitive Slave

Law of 1850, wrote a public letter sharply criticizing a proposal made by antislavery advocate Lydia Maria Child. Child had written to Governor Wise of Virginia, requesting permission to nurse John Brown in his jail cell. Mason, often quoting Scripture, condemned Child as a hypocrite for attempting to "soothe with sisterly and motherly care the hoary-headed murderer of Harper's Ferry!" Mason claimed that it was the misplaced sympathy of northern women such as Mrs. Child which contributed to the violence against innocent people perpetrated by men like Brown. Instead of offering to help Brown, Child, she said, should come to the aid of the families of his victims or minister to the less fortunate in her own neighborhood as "we do" on southern plantations. Maria Child, however, would have the last word. In a long letter of response, subsequently published in the *New York Tribune*, she told Mrs. Mason that northern women like herself already cared for the poor and comforted the sick. She then added that, after assisting the mothers in maternity, *"we do not sell the babies."*[34]

No discussion of women in pre–Civil War politics would be complete without some mention of Jane Grey Swisshelm (pronounced SWIZ-em). A native of Pennsylvania, Swisshelm became a popular newspaper reporter and editor, serving for a time as Washington correspondent for Horace Greeley's *New York Tribune* and, incidentally, opening the Senate press gallery to women. A vigorous foe of slavery, Swisshelm promoted Liberty party and Free-Soil party candidates for office in her weekly abolitionist paper, the *Pittsburgh Saturday Visitor*, in the 1840s. During the mid-1850s, Swisshelm moved west to St. Cloud, Minnesota. Named editor of the local newspaper, she began writing articles critical of the Buchanan administration and also attacked the local Democratic leadership. This strong editorializing eventually got her into deep trouble with her adversaries who destroyed her printing press. However, Swisshelm's supporters bought her a new press, and she resumed her attacks. Although Swisshelm insisted that she was not affiliated, the opposition saw her as "the mother of the Republican party" in the area. Swisshelm was originally cool to the candidacy of Abraham Lincoln in 1860 (she preferred William Seward), but took pride in the party's subsequent victory over the entrenched Democratic regime in her locale and in the nation.[35]

THE ELECTION OF 1860

Unlike Swisshelm, not all abolitionist women openly took political sides in these years. Although sympathetic to some of the goals of the

Republican party, certain female abolitionists avoided any participation in the national election of 1856 and then again in 1860. This had to do with the fact that the Republicans did not in either case come out in favor of the immediate emancipation of slaves—the party's platform had only called for stopping any further slavery expansion. However, some, like Harriet Beecher Stowe in 1860, understood that neutrality would only aid slavery's defenders and that there were definite advantages to be gained by electing Lincoln and the rest of the Republican ticket. "We are aware that the Republican party are far from being up to the full measure of what *ought* to be thought and felt on the slavery question," she noted during the campaign. "But they are for *stopping the evil*—and in this case to arrest is to cure."[36]

If extreme abolitionists had reservations and did little to promote a Republican victory, many other northern women showed no restraint in their support of the party in 1860. From the outset, pro-Republican women played an active role in the campaign, sitting in the galleries at the party convention in Chicago (Mary Livermore as a reporter would even get to sit on the convention floor), hosting barbecues, attending rallies, and marching in parades. While women through the whole northern tier of states were involved, the most enthusiastic response seems to have occurred in the West. Viewing a Republican procession in September in Kalamazoo, Michigan, an onlooker mentioned that "a new and rather significant feature was introduced into the demonstration." Some fifty young ladies on horseback, dressed in "Wide-Awake" uniforms, composed a major part of the cavalcade. A similar scene took place in the town of Porter, Michigan, where female marchers "with their sparkling eyes and flashing torches" lighted the way. The Republican Young Ladies of St. Charles, Illinois, did their part by making banners and presenting them to the town's male Wide-Awake marchers. One local woman who busied herself sewing uniforms for the paraders, after hearing that preliminary returns showed her party in the lead, declared: "I am amply repaid for all that I have done." As one partisan reporter described the notable contribution of women from the frontier states to the Republican triumph: "The brave and the true hearted girls of the West were doing their utmost for the cause of freedom."[37]

On the Democratic side, there was probably less enthusiasm and effort, owing to the sectional split in the party and the lack of good organization. Still, female supporters of Stephen Douglas marched in parades and sponsored picnics to help their party's cause. They also came in heavy numbers to the public appearances made by Douglas and his wife Adele, as the twosome gained a bit of notoriety for being the first prospective

presidential couple to travel on an extended campaign tour.[38] Douglas
also created some controversy when on the day he arrived to deliver a
speech in Springfield, Illinois, he was escorted down the main street of
town by a prominent lady, the wife of a lawyer, who had taken her
husband's carriage and put a Douglas flag on it for the occasion.[39]
Behind the scenes, women talked a lot about the contest. During the late
stages, Julia Dent Grant, wife of the soon-to-be Union general, reported
that in Illinois "there was great excitement in all political discussions."
Since Julia Grant had been a Democrat like her father, she "felt called
upon" to defend her party and its leaders whenever she heard them
assailed. It was with a "heavy heart," she later remembered, that one
evening she watched a long torchlight procession wending its way to the
courthouse. It reminded her of a great fiery serpent which within a short
time "would crush in its folds" the beloved party of her father, of
Jefferson, of General Jackson, of Thomas Benton, and of Douglas.[40]

Southern women were not as active as northern women in the 1860
presidential election partly because of traditional limits on female behavior
as well as a growing despair about the outcome. Initially, some optimism
was displayed, especially at the first Democratic National Convention in
Charleston, South Carolina, where ladies in the gallery cheered militant
southern rights' advocate William Lowndes Yancey when he addressed the
delegates. But the split in the Democratic party, after many southern
leaders refused to accept the candidacy of Stephen Douglas and then
created a separate ticket headed by John C. Breckenridge, tempered much
of the positive feeling. Further division in southern ranks caused by the
addition of John Bell and the Constitutional Union party made victory
over the Republicans seem even more doubtful. Since most men showed
no inclination to mount a vigorous campaign, women had little incentive
to do much either. While Kate Cumming of Georgia reported that at least
some women of the South were avidly reading newspapers and leaving
their homes to "attend a speech or procession," the majority remained
inactive except for deploring the selfishness of politicians and the lack
of sectional unity. The inaction persisted despite the belief of many
women of the region that Lincoln's election would seriously threaten the
southern way of life.[41]

THE SECESSION CRISIS

Yet once Lincoln's victory had occurred and the breakup of the Union
became imminent, southern women responded in a zealous manner hardly
in keeping with traditional rules of feminine behavior. In Washington,

D.C., wives of southern congressmen, "thoroughly alarmed" at the situation, began attending sessions in the House and Senate chambers to keep up with the latest developments. As reported by one of these ladies, Adele Pryor of Virginia: "From morning to the hour of adjournment we would sit spellbound, as one [speaker] after another drew the lurid picture of disunion and war." In addition, she observed, "our social lines were now strictly drawn between North and South. Names were dropped from visiting lists, occasions avoided on which we might expect to meet members of the party antagonistic to our own."[42] In late December, women packed the halls of the secession convention in Charleston, South Carolina, and screamed joyously when the decision to separate from the Union was reached. Back in Washington, the southern congressional wives cheered the announcement as "glorious news." In subsequent days, they shouted words of encouragement from the congressional galleries, when their respective husbands renounced their allegiance to the United States. Contemporaries noted how the final withdrawal of southern members awakened in these ladies "feelings of triumphant satisfaction."[43]

These and other southern women became enthusiastic promoters of secession, attending the secessionist convention in their particular state, rarely expressing any fear of the dangers that might arise as a result of the break. Convinced of the righteousness of their cause, they no less than the men boldly defended their separationist stance. "All that we ask," declared Adele Petigru Allston, wife of a South Carolina planter, is "to be allowed to govern our own Section in our own way," adding that "anyone who believes in the principles of self-government, who admits the justice of the principle for which we fought in the war of the Revolution, cannot object to our movement now."[44] In some cases, women even went further than men in demanding action. A number of female Floridians, for example, submitted a letter to a Jacksonville newspaper, denouncing the "submissive policy of southern politicians" and demanding an end to compromises with the North. The letter's authors promised to emulate "our Revolutionary matrons" and take up their spinning wheels and looms for the southern cause.[45] In the state of Alabama, an anonymous woman from Lowndes County, calling herself "Lowndes Matron," published a series of letters in the pro-secession *Montgomery Mail*, blasting "the lords of the earth" for doing nothing but talk about abolitionist wrongs. She proposed that housewives form associations for the purpose of boycotting northern manufactured goods. She also called for a boycott against local merchants who refused "to assist us in carrying out this enterprise." Soon a group known as

"Lowndes Ladies for the South" came into being and started to follow through on these proposals.[46] Presumably, similar organizations came into being elsewhere in the Deep South.

When the Confederacy was formed in February 1861, women of the South showed their patriotism in various ways. In numerous cases, they encouraged their menfolk to enlist in the armed forces and also made uniforms and collected supplies for their use. In addition, they designed flags for the new republic or made banners for local military units.[47] Besides demonstrating their ability with a needle, women in many countries competed with each other for the honor of delivering presentation speeches at a send-off ceremony just before the soldiers marched away to war. On these occasions it appears that no objections were raised against women speaking in public, and the individuals chosen seem to have taken full advantage of the opportunity to employ their rhetorical skills. Like the male orators of the day, most female speakers employed extremely florid language during their performance. Perhaps typical was a speech delivered by Miss Hassie Anderson of Pike County, Alabama, exhorting the young men of the community to

Arise, grasp your sword and wield your steel, and drive your enemies from the field. Onward, onward, you gallant band, save us! save our cherished land. Gird on your armor, lift your hearts, and God will shield you from the darts. Think of your loved ones at home . . . but not with thoughts of sad regret, your friends with love clasp you yet. God, the almighty one will save and guide the children of the brave.[48]

The war itself further politicized southern women. As historian George C. Rable has written: "The sectional conflict had stimulated awareness of public affairs, and the secession crisis had forced women of various classes to recognize the connection between public and private life. The war continued and intensified this acculturation even though women still exerted a marginal influence over government policy."[49] Women of all backgrounds developed strong opinions about particular politicians as well as military officers. While there is little evidence of direct steps taken to oust politicians they no longer favored, it is probable that some did make their negative feelings known to their menfolk. Most women urged vigorous prosecution of the war and stressed the need for southern unity. They disliked critics of Confederate president Jefferson Davis, whom they saw as the embodiment of the southern cause. However, by the last year of the war, when faced with increasing hardships, many of them changed their attitude and joined in the criticism. Women were naturally most interested in the issues that directly affected their families such as conscription and taxation. They also sent letters to government agencies regarding the disposition of their husbands or sons. Although the war did not stimulate southern women to engage in overt partisan behavior, they surely emerged from the conflict more politically minded than they had been before.[50]

The Civil War politicized women in the North just as it did in the South, although it took a while longer to reach the same level of spirit. Like their southern counterparts, northern women supported the call to battle, creating banners for local military groups and participating in send-off ceremonies. Throughout the war years, women gradually saw the need to develop greater political awareness as they realized the outcome directly affected their lives and not just those of their menfolk. "It is not enough that we scrape lint, make hospital stores, knit socks, make shirts, etc., etc.," exclaimed one Indiana woman, "we also have other duties connected with this war. . . . Let us prove that women are intellectually and morally capable of laboring side by side with our brothers in the great struggle."[51] Governmental affairs had always been seen as something outside a woman's sphere, an area "she was supposed incompetent to comprehend," declared a New Hampshirite. "But," she continued, "this painful hour of warfare crowds home upon us the conviction that woman's interests equally with man's are imperiled—private as well as public, individual as well as social."[52] In many northern communities, women joined "loyal leagues" to spur involvement by members of their sex in the war effort and to demonstrate support for the Union. Dozens of such leagues were in operation by the end of the first year.[53]

WOMEN'S WARTIME PUBLIC ACTIVITIES

Women's participation in the war effort was also promoted by speechmakers at public events and by the editors of various publications, especially women's magazines. Mainstream periodicals such as *Mother's Magazine and Family Circle* and *Godey's Lady's Book* exhorted their readers to make wartime sacrifices—engage in frugal living, care for wounded soldiers, send goods to the battle zone. They were told that they could do charitable work for the benefit of the community, but that their principal focus should still be the home. No mention was made in this type of publication about women acting in a political fashion, nor was any comment made about the government's handling of the war. Nevertheless, in a few reform-oriented journals such as *Arthur's Home Magazine* and

The Sibyl, women were encouraged to be politically aware—to read the Constitution and the addresses of prominent statesmen, as well as to understand current issues—for it was claimed women had a special role to play in forming proper community attitudes toward the war. Editorials in these publications also urged women to demand that the government vigorously pursue the fighting and to insist on the immediate overthrow of slavery.[54] It seems evident that some women were influenced by these writings, judging by the growth of female political activity by the end of the second year of the conflict.

Women's public activity took two distinct forms, following the lines advocated in the above-mentioned periodicals. The most visible type undertaken was in the area of war relief work. In April 1861, after a heavily attended rally at New York's Cooper Union, the Women's Central Association of Relief (for the Sick and Wounded of the Army) was established. This organization, which soon had several thousand branches, linked together under the auspices of the United States Sanitary Commission, provided a variety of services. Most notably, it raised funds as well as collected supplies for distribution to ailing soldiers and destitute widows and their children. It was also involved in training nurses to serve in military hospitals and in sending agents directly into the battle zone to help those in need. Undoubtedly, the women taking part made an important contribution to the war effort. But this was mainly related to the old tradition of women's benevolence.[55]

More clearly in the partisan vein was the work of the Women's National Loyal League (WNLL). The League was founded in early 1863, particularly to press for stronger action on the slavery question. Although President Lincoln had issued the Emancipation Proclamation on January 1 of that year, slavery was by no means brought to an end. The document only talked about slavery in the Confederacy and made no mention of the black bondage that continued to exist in Union-held territory. In order to prod the Lincoln administration toward immediate abolition of slavery everywhere, WNLL organizers Elizabeth Cady Stanton and Susan B. Anthony focused on sending a massive petition to Congress containing one million signatures from all over the Union. Appealing both to women already associated with antislavery societies and those not yet institutionally involved, Stanton and Anthony emphasized the moral nature of the slavery question and argued that it fell within women's proper bounds for action. However, they did not find it easy to gain adherents. Many abolitionist-minded women felt uncomfortable with the intrusion into national politics. Some also seemed disturbed by the mixing of antislavery and feminism, which the leaders had encouraged by introducing resolutions linking race and gender. In the end, only about 5,000 women fully joined the national organization, and less than half the desired number of signatures were ever obtained. Yet the fact that petitions were compiled with more than 400,000 names—two-thirds from women—illustrates the success of this project. It also shows that women's political activity did not stop during the war.[56]

The presidential contest of 1864 would give abolitionist and women's rights activists like Stanton and Anthony a further opportunity to encourage women's participation in politics. They realized that if women played an active part in the election, it would demonstrate that women deserved full citizenship rights after the war. In advertising the second annual convention of the WNLL that spring, Stanton and Anthony urged women to attend and "make themselves a *Power for Freedom* in the coming Presidential Campaign." Actually, the two leaders hoped to use the convention to promote the prospective candidacy of John C. Frémont, who had taken a stronger abolitionist stance than Lincoln early in the war. However, their approach was criticized in many quarters, even among antislavery women. In a letter published in the *Liberator*, Caroline Dall of Boston told Stanton that the WNLL meeting should not be turned into an "electioneering caucus," and that women should limit their interests to the "moral aspects of government." Stanton replied that the Loyal League was committed to a political purpose and that the future of both women and the slaves was at stake in the 1864 election. Women, she warned, should not wait for an invitation before entering the political arena, for "aristocracy never seeks to share its privileges." Stanton also pointed to women's past involvement in partisan politics since the election of 1840 as a means of establishing precedents for her proposed actions. As it turned out, because of various behind-the-scenes pressures the WNLL leaders chose to restrain themselves and the convention did not become an "electioneering caucus." In addition, the Frémont candidacy, though supported by some male and female abolitionists for a while, eventually petered out.[57] Nevertheless, women would play a more prominent role than in any previous presidential campaign, and would deliver quite a number of public speeches for the occasion.

WOMEN LECTURERS

The foremost figure on the political lecture circuit in 1864 was Anna E. Dickinson of Pennsylvania. Dickinson, a twenty-two-year-old Quaker woman, had first attracted national attention three years earlier, having deeply stirred a large abolitionist gathering in Philadelphia with her powerful oratory. While not too sympathetic toward President Lincoln and his party at the outset because of their less than vigorous conduct of the war and slow movement on the slavery question, Dickinson gradually came to the administration's support. As Republican politicians heard her lectures "melt audiences to tears," they began employing her in several statewide campaigns. She was particularly effective in the New England state elections of 1863, swaying voters against the Democrats to prevent the Democrats from regaining control of New Hampshire and Connecticut. New Hampshire's governor-elect personally acknowledged that her eloquent speeches secured him his triumph, and Connecticut's Republican state chairman declared that as an orator, "she has no equal."[58] In January 1864, Dickinson took the unprecedented step of addressing a joint session of Congress, urging the need for greater progress toward victory in the war. Although still cool toward the president, she campaigned in Pennsylvania and New York later that year for Lincoln's reelection, condemning his opponent General George McClellan in the strongest terms. After the war, Dickinson abandoned politics for a more lucrative lecturing and stage career, but she did at times return to the stump during future presidential campaigns.[59]

Dickinson's success on the campaign trail encouraged the Democrats to employ their own female orators. New Orleans-born Emma Webb, who had been an actress on the New York stage since 1860, challenged Dickinson's views first in a speech at the Cooper Union in April 1864 and then on several subsequent occasions. Webb defended slavery as the proper status for the black man and applauded General McClellan for his prudent course in fighting the Confederacy. She also praised "Copperhead" leader Clement Vallandigham of Ohio for his stance on the war, calling for an immediate end to hostilities and a return to the prewar status quo. Another Democratic speaker was Terese Esmond, an Irish-American woman, who also railed against Dickinson's "rampant abolitionism and abuse of McClellan." On the Republican side, Cordelia Phillips gave a number of speeches while campaigning for "Abe and Andy" [Lincoln and Johnson] in the late stages of the presidential race. Her speeches were said to have been "fairly well written and pretty effectively delivered," but she lacked the oratorical power of Anna Dickinson. By election day, the acceptance of women as political lecturers was far from complete. Some critics saw them as motivated simply by vanity or monetary gain. Others concluded that people were fools to go listen to them.[60] Yet regardless of this initial response, women platform speakers gradually became a standard feature of political campaigns over the next few decades.

Indeed, in the years prior to and during the Civil War, women particularly in the northern states would begin to make a more conspicuous place for themselves in the partisan political world. Although not usually at the center of things, they were a growing presence. Drawn into the fray either because of their interest in reform or because of strong sectional leanings, women were increasingly active in campaigns and in public acts related to the breakup of the Union and to the war itself. While some men may still have complained about women's participation, it was becoming clear that up to a certain level their political involvement was increasingly acceptable, and women themselves were growing more comfortable in that expanding role.

Chapter 4

The Postwar Decades: Suffrage and Politics

In the postwar period, increasing numbers of American women hoped to play a greater role in the political realm. Although the majority of both sexes probably still felt that women did not belong in politics, prewar and wartime experiences had politicized many more members of the female sex than in past generations, and surely a considerable percentage wished to maintain their political connections or even enhance them. Reformers of all kinds wanted to use their established ties to help carry out further reforms. Others caught up in the ongoing conflict between Republicans and Democrats had no desire to sever their links as the party struggle continued. However, some women's rights advocates became ambivalent toward the major parties not too long afterward when neither of them, despite some encouraging words on the subject, proved willing to take any tangible steps to promote female suffrage.

AGITATION FOR THE VOTE

Clearly one sign of women's desire to be included in the political process in the early postwar years was the growing demand for equal suffrage. Women reformers who had contributed to the war effort in various ways truly believed that the men in power should reward the female half of the population for their service. As the now dominant Republican party had come to see the justice and necessity of granting recently freed black men full citizenship status, many of these women concluded that the party ought to do the same for them. While some members of Congress undoubtedly agreed, when it came time to formally consider the matter, party leaders together with prominent male abolition-ists rejected this course. They claimed that this was the "Negro's hour" and that it would be too difficult politically to gain approval of both black and women's voting rights at the same moment. Even certain advocates of suffrage equality such as Lucy Stone reluctantly accepted this argument and assumed that once black men got the vote the enfranchisement of women would not be far behind.[1]

Elizabeth Cady Stanton and Susan B. Anthony were less optimistic, convinced that the Constitution with the proposed Fifteenth Amendment, by specifically giving black *men* voting rights, would be explicitly disfran-chising all women. This led to a major split in the recently formed woman suffrage movement. Stanton and Anthony created a separate group, the National Woman Suffrage Association (NWSA), distancing itself from individuals like Stone, who subsequently formed the American Woman Suffrage Association (AWSA), and also splitting from the Republican party. For a time, the NWSA seemed to favor the opposition Democrats; Anthony even served as a delegate to the Democratic National Convention in 1868. She tried to encourage the idea among the party leadership that if their side backed equal suffrage the new female voters would become steadfast supporters of the Democratic party. However, the Democrats, both those at the top and the rank-in-file, refused to go along. Still dependent on their urban immigrant and southern base, they were clearly less comfortable with women's presence in the political sphere than the Republicans and never went as far as their rivals in seriously considering suffrage reform.[2]

THE GROWING SUFFRAGE DEBATE

The postwar debate on voting rights again brought up questions about women's suitability for the hard-nosed political world. Horace Bushnell, one of the leading Protestant ministers of the day, probably echoed the majority feeling among males when he called female suffrage a reform against nature. Like earlier religious spokesmen, Bushnell argued that God had ordained men and women to perform separate functions and duties on earth. He also emphasized that women's different biology and supposedly greater emotionality made them unfit for the rigors of politics.

The active campaigning work of political life, is certainly in quite too high a key for the delicate organization, and the fearfully exciteable susceptibilities of women. They have no conception now, as they look on, of the gustiness and high tempest their frail skiffs must encounter. The struggle is a trial even for men, that sometimes quite overturns their self-mastery, and totally breaks down the strength both of their principles and their bodies. And yet if we enlarge the contest, as we must, when we bring in women, it will be manifold more intense than now.

Bushnell also claimed that the inclusion of women in all aspects of partisan political activity "will ultimately dissolve the bonds of delicacy and the proprieties of good manners" between the sexes.[3]

The editor of the *New York Tribune*, Horace Greeley, was somewhat more sympathetic to women's political input; though totally negative to the idea of equal suffrage, he offered a proposal allowing female participation but on a separate and limited basis. Greeley claimed that, although their influence on legislation and government policy should be felt, if women entered the system as presently constituted, it would end up corrupting them rather than reforming men and improving politics. "We only insist that she shall speak and distinctly be heard as woman, not mingled and confused with men," he declared. Greeley recommended setting aside certain areas of legislation for women, that is, matters relating to the family, including marriage, divorce, maintenance of children, education, and women's property rights. Under Greeley's plan, women would not go to the polls and cast regular ballots. Instead, qualified women in each state assembly district would mail in ballots, the results to be tabulated by a local woman's organization and a decision rendered. This method, he thought, would be less costly than regular voting and would also allow the invalid, the bedridden, and the bereaved to participate. Most importantly, it would permit women to legislate in some fields and still retain the "time honored distinctions between men and women."[4] Greeley's plan was, of course, unacceptable to woman suffragists who saw that it would still make them second-class citizens and, in fact, would place them in a position that would seem to legitimize their alleged inferiority.

Not all male political leaders opposed equal suffrage. Some recognized the valuable service women had already rendered, and believed, either for idealistic or partisan reasons, that they could make an even greater contribution if given the opportunity. One of these men was Republican Senator Oliver P. Morton of Indiana, a loyal party player on most issues during the Reconstruction era. In a speech before his senatorial colleagues in the early 1870s, Morton openly called for equal suffrage, bluntly answering the familiar charge that women would be corrupted by going to the polling place. On the contrary, he asserted, it "would make the polls more decent, more respectable than they are now." He also mentioned that fifty years earlier the idea of women attending political meetings was "intolerable to a great many people. . . . But now women go to political meetings. In almost every canvass in my state there are nearly as many women who attend the meetings as men." He added that women's presence "elevates the character of these meetings" and "has made them more respectable."[5] Yet Morton's words would fail to sway the majority either in or out of Congress. Most men of the time refused to acknowledge women's already conspicuous part in politics and showed no willingness to yield on the matter of the vote. The debate over woman suffrage would continue. Indeed, it would go on for almost another half-century, though during that time women would keep on attending partisan political meetings and taking on other political roles long before the question of the vote was finally resolved.

WOMEN IN NATIONAL POLITICS

Just as was the case earlier, some women on the national scene went to considerable lengths in trying to get their menfolk chosen president—and themselves first lady of the land. In fact, prior to the election of 1868, one of them even got herself deeply involved in the nominating process. Kate Chase Sprague, the beautiful and ambitious daughter of Supreme Court justice and former Lincoln cabinet member Salmon P. Chase, worked hard to obtain the nomination of her father, who had received a few overtures from the Democrats to become their standard-bearer. She became the first woman ever to play an active role at a party nominating convention. Although barred from the convention floor, she spent a good deal of time at private caucuses, meeting with delegates, hoping to create a groundswell of support for her father's candidacy. But despite all her electioneering, the scheme to nominate Chase did not get very far, because many southerners had no wish to align themselves with someone of his antislavery background.[6] More successful in getting her man elected that year was Julia Grant, wife of the victorious Union general and Republican nominee Ulysses Grant. Although Grant undoubtedly would have won the presidency even without an openly supportive mate, surely her actions proved helpful. When the campaign first started, Julia recalled, she was not too happy facing all the "receptions of committees, regiments of soldiers, serenades, delegations from north, east, south, and west, and from every state of the Union." Yet being "intensely interested in the success of our ticket," she "became an enthusiastic politician. No delegation was too large, no serenade too long." Even when her husband began to be criticized by the press, she, "like the General . . . grew not to mind it."[7]

Julia Grant was not alone in serving as political wife and confidante of an ambitious husband in the postwar period. Another who stood out in this role was Mary Logan of Illinois. Married at seventeen to John Logan, a lawyer twelve years her senior, Mary Logan willingly accompanied her husband on his early campaigns for the state legislature and for Congress. During the war, when John Logan was appointed an army commander in Tennessee, she went with him and handled many administrative matters concerning nurse recruitment and supplies. Following the war, after her husband became head of the newly established veterans group, the Grand Army of the Republic (GAR), Mary Logan was active in founding the women's auxiliary of the GAR. Later she assisted her husband in many ways during his years as a U.S. senator and in his quest for the vice-presidency in 1884. She was said to be the most politically astute woman of the age—well known for her charm and tact as well as for her knowledge of current affairs. Unlike many of her sex who felt ill at ease making public appearances, Mary Logan could handle any such situation. At one stop on their national campaign tour in 1884, when her husband was too hoarse to make any statement to members of the press, Mary spoke to them and to many callers, "volunteering information and answering questions with an easy grace that made all feel 'at home.'"[8]

FIRST PURSUIT OF OFFICE

Although acceptance of women into the political sphere remained a slow process, some progress was made regarding female appointments to jobs in the federal bureaucracy and to other patronage posts previously confined to men. In Washington, D.C., the number of women in government departments rose dramatically from the start of the Civil War to 1900. Before the war, only a handful had been so employed, but by 1872 there were 400 women in the Treasury Department and nearly as many in other agencies such as the Patent Office, the Census Bureau, and the Department of the Interior. Despite some opposition by traditionalists who felt women did not belong in such posts, the trend continued. By the year 1900, some 7,500 of the 27,600 (27 percent) government workers were women.[9] Around the country, the political parties, to reward individuals for past service, designated many additional female postmasters (i.e., postmistresses), and certain state organizations chose a few women to work for the legislature. For example, in Iowa, in 1870, the Republican-dominated lower house hired its first female clerk, Mary Spencer of Clinton County. Perhaps an even bigger breakthrough involved the placing of women on important state boards for the first time. A major instance of this was the appointment of the highly respected reformer Josephine Shaw Lowell to the New York State Board of Charities by Democratic Governor Samuel Tilden in 1876.[10]

Not only were women being designated to appointive offices, but some also started thinking about seeking elective offices. Even before the postwar conflict over the suffrage heated up, Elizabeth Cady Stanton in 1866 became the first of her sex to run for a seat in Congress partly in order to test a woman's constitutional right to do so. Apparently, no such limitation existed, so Stanton, a resident of the Eighth Congressional District in upstate New York, issued a public letter announcing herself as a candidate. In that letter, she criticized both major parties for what she considered their principal shortcomings, proclaiming herself an Independent and a supporter of women's rights. The *New York Herald*, though perhaps not with total sincerity, advocated her election, saying: "A lady of fine presence and accomplishments in the House of Representatives would wield a wholesome influence over the rough and disorderly elements of that body." It is not clear whether Stanton seriously campaigned for the position. The results show that she received only 24 of the 22,050 votes cast, but she was not dismayed by the low level of support. Looking back on the experience, Stanton said her only regret was not having photographs of these two dozen "unknown friends."[11]

The early 1870s saw the appearance of the first female presidential candidate—the notorious and highly unconventional Victoria Woodhull. Woodhull, who grew up in a family of spiritualists, had little formal education but possessed striking beauty along with a magnetic personality. She married several times, the first time at age fifteen. For years she was involved in traveling medicine shows, holding seances, and living an altogether unorthodox lifestyle for the nineteenth century. Then, after moving to New York City, Victoria, together with her sister Tennessee Claflin, developed a friendship with wealthy railroad magnate Cornelius Vanderbilt, and through his help achieved quick success in the stock market. Still surrounded by spiritualists, Woodhull became an advocate of many controversial reforms, including "free love," which she promoted in her own newspaper. Her interest in full female equality soon attracted her to the suffrage question. An excellent public speaker, Woodhull became the first of her sex to address a congressional committee in Washington, D.C. (1871), arguing that women as American citizens under the recently amended Constitution should already be qualified as voters. Initially encouraging her to go further in this cause, a number of suffragists led by Susan B. Anthony eventually saw Woodhull's shortcomings, especially her lack of stability, and abruptly cut off all connections with her.

But their snub did not stop Woodhull and those around her from pursuing a rather grandiose plan. They encouraged her remaining followers to form a separate group known as the Equal Rights party, who proceeded to nominate her for the presidency of the United States. Woodhull's unprecedented candidacy, however, barely got off the ground, as legal and financial problems, along with a hostile press, prevented her from carrying on much of a campaign. By the first week of November, the so-called Mrs. Satan was arrested on somewhat questionable charges and put in jail. Although Woodhull was soon released and continued to address the subject of equal rights for women, she no longer exerted much public influence after that time.[12]

However one assesses Woodhull's overall impact, her statements did raise important questions about women's rights. In addition, she helped popularize a view of politics held by many of her contemporaries and by later feminists—that women should pursue an independent course and not attach themselves to either of the major parties. Both of them, she declared, had prostituted "the whole power of the government to their own selfish purposes." Women, she felt, should be something more than Democrats or Republicans, and bring a higher moral force into governmental affairs. These ideas did not originate with Woodhull. From the late 1860s, leaders of the National Woman Suffrage Association such as Stanton and Anthony, seeing that the major parties and even minor parties were not truly interested in wide-ranging reform that included woman suffrage, had begun thinking about following a different course. In May 1872, when the Association met in New York City, a measure was introduced urging the creation of a new political party "whose principles shall meet the issues of the hour, and represent equal rights for all." Such a party could lay the basis for an "honest administration," one that would eliminate "political and social abuses," as well as work for "the emancipation of labor" and "the enfranchisement of women." Yet the convention delegates, after discussing the proposal at length, came to realize that it was one thing to talk about a separate party but another to launch it in a truly meaningful way.[13]

THE ELECTION OF 1872

Lucy Stone and her followers in the American Woman Suffrage Association had already rejected the idea of forming an independent party. They continued to believe that the Republicans offered the best chance for progressive change, including woman suffrage. Even most members of the National Woman Suffrage Association eventually backed the Republican national ticket in 1872 when they looked at the alternative. The opposition—comprised of the Democratic party and the new Liberal Republican group—had both nominated ardent suffrage foe Horace Greeley for president and made no mention of women's rights in their platforms. Meanwhile, the Republican standard-bearer Ulysses Grant seemed somewhat open to the possibility of woman suffrage, and his running mate, Henry Wilson, was a known supporter of the cause. Moreover, the GOP national convention, after hearing a plea from Lucy Stone's husband Henry Blackwell, for the first time adopted a resolution about women's status, which seemed to open the door a slight degree toward greater equality. It stated: "The Republican party is mindful of its obligations to the loyal women of America for their noble devotion to the cause of freedom; their admission to wider fields of usefulness is viewed with satisfaction and the honest demand of any class of citizens for additional rights, should be treated with respectful consideration."[14]

As a result, the leaders of the NWSA, ignoring the Grant administration's dismal first-term record, issued a long, impassioned statement calling on the women of America to "lay aside our party preferences" and forget the unfulfilled Republican commitments of the past. It was necessary, they said, to get involved and "throw our whole influence of pen and voice into this campaign." Local woman suffrage organizations in particular were asked to hold mass meetings in all the large cities of their respective states; to cooperate with official Republican committees; to send into each election district the best women speakers; and to circulate documents throughout every school district. In every possible way, women were supposed to "throw the whole weight of their influence on the side of the Republican party."[15] Lucy Stone and the AWSA temporarily stopped their feud with the NWSA and collaborated in the effort to defeat Greeley. Urging unity among her sex, Stone exclaimed: "Let every State be canvassed by women speakers and roused by woman's influence. Let the election of Grant and Wilson be a triumph of civilization, a monument of the cordial cooperation of American men and women for the welfare of mankind and the establishment of Equal Rights for All."[16]

The Republican National Committee, seeking to capitalize on the talents of these well-known women, soon published thousands of copies of this appeal and had them distributed countrywide. It also brought Susan B. Anthony to Washington to consult at length with the committee on the best way to achieve the desired goals. Anthony readily offered the services of leading suffragists to hold public gatherings and go on speaking tours in behalf of the Republican candidates. Her proposals for the campaign were quickly agreed upon, and both the National and New York state GOP committees put ample funds at her disposal for a series of meetings all over the Empire State. In addition, Mary Livermore, Elizabeth Cady Stanton, and other prominent advocates of women's rights agreed to take part in the canvass in Connecticut and Pennsylvania. Stanton later told Anthony that she would rather have Beelzebub chosen president than Horace Greeley.[17]

Altogether, at least forty notable women were galvanized for the battle between Grant and Greeley. Throughout September and October, this phalanx of women went on the stump, a far cry from the mere handful who appeared during the Lincoln-McClellan race eight years earlier. Often two or three of them spoke at the same meeting. On October 5 in Rochester, New York, Elizabeth Cady Stanton, along with suffragists Matilda Gage and Olympia Brown, appeared before an audience of several thousand. In Charlestown, Massachusetts, a day earlier, Lucy Stone, ordained minister Ada Bowles, and black author Frances Harper addressed an equally large crowd. Harper, born a free black in Maryland, encouraged her listeners to support the Republican party, which she saw as "an evangel of freedom," and claimed not one Democrat could be found among colored women in the former Confederate states. In the Midwest, the Republican cause was most ably served by a young spellbinder named Matilda Fletcher of Council Bluffs, Iowa, who spoke almost daily for two months in Ohio, Indiana, and Nebraska, as well as in her native state. A high-level Republican official later said of Fletcher: "No other speaker made a more popular canvass or contributed more to the glorious results."[18] Across the continent in Oregon, Abigail Scott Duniway, editor of the *New Northwest*, a woman suffrage paper, placed the names of Grant and Wilson in bold letters at the top of its columns. Both in print and in public lectures, Duniway told why they should be supported over Greeley and his running mate, B. Gratz Brown. Assessing female participation in the Republican campaign, one spokesman asserted that "women were taking an active part in the political questions of the day, and were received with enthusiasm wherever they appeared."[19]

Horace Greeley had only one prominent woman orator on his side: Anna Dickinson. Although Dickinson had always favored the Republicans and been an advocate of women's rights, she, like many other Americans, did not believe Grant deserved a second term and so she came out for Greeley. The Greeley campaign organization, however, failed to take much advantage of Dickinson's renowned speaking talents, although it did schedule her for one major address at New York City's Cooper Union in late October. There, before a packed audience, Dickinson gave a masterful speech, condemning the flagrant corruption of the Grant regime and its inadequate Reconstruction policy. As for Greeley's indifference to woman suffrage, Dickinson claimed that it was more important for the time being to back a candidate who stood for integrity, justice, and humanity. Dickinson's speech won rave reviews from impartial observers, but being delivered as it was near the end of the campaign it swayed few voters.[20] Her contribution, moreover, could not compare with the scores of female activists on the opposing side. In Massachusetts, for example, Lucy Stone and many others delivered speeches, wrote newspaper articles, and did a great deal of canvassing. As one participant summed it up, Republican women "did as much effective work during the campaign as if each one had been a 'man and a voter.' They did everything but vote."[21] Yet in the end all these efforts did not bring women any closer to becoming enfranchised; after Grant won the election, the Republican leadership postponed any action on the matter indefinitely.

DISILLUSIONMENT WITH THE REPUBLICANS

In subsequent years, as Republican indifference showed no signs of fading, some suffrage advocates concluded that they should refrain from supporting either party in the foreseeable future. There was the feeling that until the major parties showed real evidence of moving forward on the suffrage issue women should simply take a nonpartisan stance. As Mary B. Clay, a leading suffragist from Kentucky, later described her disillusionment with the Republicans: "I do not believe in women allowing themselves to be used as they have been for years by that party for its own advancement, and then, when its ends are attained it has ignored all petitions for woman's elevation."[22] Others, however, disagreed with this point of view and reluctantly concluded that partisan attachment offered the only hope for eventual approval, and so they sought to prod the parties in the same mode as earlier. They promised everlasting loyalty to the one that championed equal suffrage, and claimed that having women on its side would ensure permanent dominance. "Whichever party enfranchise Woman . . . will make a brilliant strategical stroke," read one suffragist memorial of the time.[23] The choice between taking a partisan or nonpartisan position was especially difficult for former abolitionists like Lucy Stone. Stone had long favored the Republicans for their anti-slave and pro-freedmen's policies, but now started questioning that allegiance as the party seemed to be abandoning what she thought was its pledge to women.

Stone and other Massachusetts suffragists hoped for a turnabout in 1876. But when the state's GOP convention that year refused once more to back women's voting rights, her group bolted and endorsed a separate pro-suffrage ticket for statewide offices. "We owe it as much to our self respect as to the principle we advocate," declared Stone, "to accept the broken pledges of the Republican party and their avowed duplicity to our cause, as abundant proof that hereafter, suffragists cannot depend on that party."[24] To be sure, Stone and her followers still had some affection for the party's national slate headed by Rutherford B. Hayes, a man who privately sympathized with the suffragists' goal. Moreover, four years later, at the start of the 1880 presidential campaign, Stone insisted that if she herself could cast a vote in this contest, she would give it "under present circumstances" to the Republican party. Yet further on in the same statement, Stone appeared to be leaning in another direction, insisting that "the great need of the age, in a truly representative government, requires a political organization different from either the Republican or the Democratic parties." She admitted that each of the two major parties had helped expand political rights in the past. The Democrats had launched the drive against property qualifications for voters, while the Republicans had freed the slaves and enfranchised the freedmen. But, she exclaimed, there were still 12 million unenfranchised women in the country held by this government "as conquerors hold their subjects."[25]

Nevertheless, Stone's talk of a new party proved to be short-lived, and in 1884, she came back to the Republican fold once more. The shift was prompted by startling revelations about the private life of Democratic presidential candidate Grover Cleveland. In that election, Cleveland, the reform governor of New York, had as his opponent James G. Blaine, the Republican senator from Maine. Blaine was known to have been involved in a number of shady political and financial deals, which had alienated many members of his own party, including Stone's close friend and pro-suffrage ally Thomas Wentworth Higginson. Yet shortly after the contest began it was revealed that the bachelor Cleveland, several years earlier, had engaged in an illicit affair with a young woman and had sired an illegitimate son. To Stone and many other women suffragists with strong moral convictions, Cleveland's personal behavior seemed infinitely worse than anything Blaine might have done in the public sphere. They felt they could not remain politically neutral but must join with the Republicans to keep Cleveland out of the White House. "We must regard the effort to place him at the head of the government, as an indignity offered to the women of this nation which ought not soon to be forgotten," wrote one of Stone's allies.[26] Stone herself stated that "women must be opposed, at all other cost, to that which is the destruction of the home. They know with an unerring instinct that the purity and safety of the home means purity and safety to the State and Nation."[27] The thrust of the criticism, however, did not sway too many male voters and Cleveland won due to other factors. Although Stone did not resurrect the issue when Cleveland ran again for the presidency in 1888 and 1892, presumably she, like her pro-Republican husband Henry Blackwell, favored the election of GOP nominee Benjamin Harrison in those years.

Like Lucy Stone, Susan B. Anthony also had an ongoing though often strained relationship with the Republicans. In fact, Anthony grew less attached to the party than Stone, as time passed and the possibility of congressional action for equal suffrage diminished. Yet despite being treated with indifference by the GOP national convention in 1880 and receiving a noncommital response from party nominee James Garfield, she did not sever her allegiance.[28] She remained somewhat sympathetic toward the Republicans (privately, if not always publicly) and refused to consider supporting any third parties during the next dozen years. Some of those parties had gone as far as to endorse suffrage reform and give women recognition at their conventions. But Anthony felt that as long as those organizations had no national clout and elected no congressmen, women who backed them would always be involved in a futile exercise. She knew that almost half the Republicans in Congress probably favored woman suffrage, and that, for her, represented a good reason to continue offering at least some praise for their candidates and policies. When asked to go against the GOP in 1888, Miss Anthony, referring to the franchise, replied: "I do not propose to work for the defeat of the party which thus far has furnished nearly every vote in that direction."[29] At times her Republicanism became fully active, such as in the 1892 campaign, when she made a three-week speaking tour of Kansas, hoping that state party leaders would be grateful and get behind a suffrage referendum. But when this did not happen Anthony returned to a nonpartisan stance, privately criticizing those women who continued to act as "Spaniels & lick the hand that smites us." Anthony briefly worked with the Populists in 1894 after they had declared their support of women's voting rights. But when that party merged with the Democrats in the election of 1896 and the topic was dropped, the now legendary reformer reaffirmed her neutral position, saying that she would not speak out for any party until it moved favorably on the suffrage issue.[30]

Two other notable women activists of the time completely broke away from the Republican camp at a relatively early stage, and with changing circumstances supported a variety of other parties. Elizabeth Cady Stanton, after backing Ulysses Grant for the presidency in 1872, switched along with the rest of her family to reform-minded Democrat Samuel Tilden in 1876. By 1888 Stanton, a longtime temperance advocate, came out for the Prohibitionists, finding in its platform "more promise of social reorganization than in either of the others," and in 1896, saw Democrat-Populist candidate William Jennings Bryan as the best choice. Although we cannot be certain, she presumably supported Bryan again in 1900 as her daughter Harriot did. Mary Livermore, former teacher, abolitionist, wartime administrator, and suffragist ally of Lucy Stone in Massachusetts, followed a slightly different path. A staunch Republican in the early 1870s, Livermore became an active member of the Prohibition movement over the next decade and publicly promoted the Prohibitionist ticket. Then, in the last years of her life, influenced by the writings of Edward Bellamy, she drifted toward Christian socialism.[31]

FURTHER PURSUIT OF OFFICE

One longtime suffragist who got no satisfaction from the Republicans felt the answer was to follow in Victoria Woodhull's footsteps and become an independent candidate for president. Belva Lockwood, a Washington, D.C., lawyer, who for many years had been an ardent advocate for women's rights and the first woman to argue a case before the U.S. Supreme Court, reintroduced the idea of a separate woman's ticket in the summer of 1884. After attending the Republican National Convention that June and being unable to get the resolutions (platform) committee to offer legal recognition to those of her gender, Lockwood wrote an impassioned public letter asking why women should not be nominated and elected to important positions in government. "If women . . . are not permitted to vote, there is no law against them being voted for," Lockwood declared. Soon she accepted the nomination for the nation's highest office by a small group of suffragists who, like Woodhull's one-time supporters, called themselves the Equal Rights party. Lockwood's candidacy was more than just a symbolic one, and she took every aspect seriously. In her platform, she claimed that she would seek to ensure a fair distribution of public offices "to women as well as to men." Concerned with the politically powerless in society, Lockwood said she would work for the soldier's widow and orphan, and obtain citizenship for the Indians. Moreover, she insisted that she would oppose wholesale monopoly of the judiciary by the male sex and would appoint a competent woman to any vacancy that occurred on the federal bench, including the Supreme Court.[32]

Although mocked by reporters and ridiculed by young men—marching groups sometimes staged mock political processions in major cities, parading around in Mother Hubbard dresses and poke bonnets[33]—Lockwood campaigned vigorously. In her many speeches, she focused on the idea of equal suffrage, saying that "contrary to the Bill of Rights," women were being governed "without their consent." Yet despite her valiant efforts, she failed to convert more than a handful of males. Even most leading female activists refused to support her. Susan B. Anthony believed that Lockwood's candidacy like Woodhull's would hurt rather than help the suffrage cause. Lockwood, of course, disagreed, asserting that "the establishment of the principles that a woman may be nominated and elected President of the United States" was calculated to do "a vast amount of good." If her party could get just one vote in the electoral college, the campaign would become "the entering wedge," she added. In the final count, Lockwood received only 4,149 votes in the six states where her name was on the ballot. But if she was disappointed she did not show it. Four years later, she ran again, though this time she obtained even fewer votes. Nevertheless, Lockwood was content to have made America more conscious of "women's right to political equality," and she correctly noted that "women in politics have come to stay."[34]

Belva Lockwood's quest for the presidency in the 1880s was certainly a unique effort, but she did not stand alone as a female office-seeker at the time. Whether spurred by her actions or merely by their eligibility to serve in certain posts, women began breaking other barriers, running for offices high and low. Some ran on Equal Rights party tickets in a few states, and others as independents. In 1888, the Equal Rights party in New York held a convention and nominated reformer Linda Gilbert for governor (though a male reporter covering the event dwelled more on the fact that the party secretary had seemingly lost the platform proceedings). In South Carolina that year, Miss Eliza Garner of Union County became the first woman candidate of any kind in her state's history, as she ran for the post of county commissioner. After receiving only forty votes in the Democratic primary, Garner decided to run as an independent but again she did not fare very well.[35] In most places where women sought office at this juncture, they tended to run for the school board or school commissioner's job, partly because these were felt to be the only suitable positions for women and partly because women had become eligible in some states to elect people to those positions.

For women candidates, even in the races for school commissioner or superintendent, winning an election was no easy task. The experience of Sarah Christie Stevens, a Minnesota farm woman, running for the post of superintendent in Mankato County in 1890, highlights the kinds of difficulties women faced. Right from the start, she failed to obtain the nomination from either of the major parties, although she did wind up with the backing of two minor ones. As the campaign proceeded, her correspondence shows her seeking the endorsement of influential men in her community and then, like male politicians, making "horse trades" for votes. Since the idea of a woman campaigning for office was so unconventional at the time, Sarah Stevens, when speaking in public, tried to allay fears by emphasizing that someone of her sex could perform in a public position without losing her womanly graces. She also claimed she had no desire to be a career politician, and wished only to serve the public faithfully in the designated job. Perhaps because she was a woman office-seeker, Mrs. Stevens received a sharp personal attack from her Republican opponent. However, the strategy apparently backfired as many "chivalric" male voters came to her defense. Stevens also had the support of Civil War veterans since as a young woman she had served the Union cause as a volunteer nurse. Of course, she had extensive female support, but curiously it was much stronger in rural areas than in urban centers. (This may have reflected the relatively greater strength of the major parties in the cities.) In any case, Stevens finally won in a three-way race and evidently performed satisfactorily as superintendent since she was re-elected four years later.[36]

DEEPENING POLITICAL INVOLVEMENT

While a few women sought office and some established a partisan connection through the suffrage movement, the majority of those who became politically active simply got caught up in the excitement of the postwar party struggle. In contrast to former times, their participation was more likely to come about voluntarily rather than through male recruitment. This era has often been characterized as the "golden age of parties," and more women than ever joined the festivities, particularly in national election years. In 1876, one commentator noted that the presidential campaign was "waking up the attention, and engaging the sympathies of women all over the land" to a greater extent than at any time since the war period. Not only was the growth quantitative but qualitative. Thomas Wentworth Higginson, a leading reformer, claimed that women were taking a "more intelligent interest" than in the past. Lincoln and Grant, he said, had been supported mainly out of loyalty and sentiment. Now, women had begun to seriously study the issues. They also revived the idea, which originated in the 1840s, of forming separate women's groups to help the candidates of their choice. One such organization was the Ladies' Garfield and Arthur Club in Cincinnati, Ohio in 1880. Its officers stated that "we, as women, who do have political opinions and partisan preferences and desire to manifest them in every manner compatible with womanly modesty, honor, integrity and our limited rights, have organized ourselves into a club to aid the election of James A. Garfield as President and Chester A. Arthur as Vice President of the United States, hoping that our efforts may be of service to the Republican party."[37]

Women's deepening political involvement as this era wore on was becoming evident to a growing number of men. Colonel Albert Clarke of Massachusetts, who spoke at a statewide suffrage association gathering in 1890, declared that "women hear politics discussed, and they read newspapers. In presidential, and often in other campaigns, they attend political meetings. In many cases they even form political clubs. They understand the issues as well as men do, and they take as much interest in the result."[38] Women's campaign input in these years was similarly noticed by foreign observers such as the Englishman, Lord James Bryce, author of what became a classic analysis of political life in the United States, *The American Commonwealth*. Women in this country, he said, though not always committed at the start, often ended up drawn "into the vortex" by "the excitement of a close struggle." Receptions for the candidates were organized "by the ladies of each party" and were reported to the press as "politically significant." Bryce also mentioned that quite a few letters in the newspapers on political subjects "bear female signatures."[39]

Who were the women active in partisan politics at this time? Those involved in organizing events and attending meetings were mainly urban women of the middle and upper classes, who had at least some education. In a way it was perhaps inevitable that they be of these classes since any individuals active in partisan politics could not be too heavily burdened with daily chores. Unlike the situation in the early 1840s, when factory women occasionally campaigned against particular legislators, there seems little evidence of female labor participation at this point. Although certain women who marched in parades and cheered at rallies may have been of working-class background, the well-to-do were rather conspicuous in any type of activity beyond this. Besides having some degree of affluence, a considerable percentage of the participants were probably married, though some single women from wealthy families obviously had the leisure time for political pursuits. The majority present at meetings must have been married, as is evident from comments made by male speakers praising the mothers in the audience and from a remark made by Michigan Senator Zachariah Chandler at a Republican rally telling women married to "Copperhead" husbands to learn to sleep alone.[40]

Women's behavior at political meetings attended by persons of both sexes is not easily discerned, inasmuch as few descriptions characterize their conduct. However, one account of a mixed gathering in Chicago at the start of the 1880 campaign indicates that they were highly attentive and knowledgeable, and at least as responsive as the men to what was being said.

> The galleries were occupied by an assemblage that would have done honor to grand opera on the occasion of the prima donna's benefit. Nearly one-half was composed of ladies, young and old, in the most of cases in evening dress, and they were eager listeners to the polished periods of General Woodford and the cutting sarcasms of Judge Thomas Tourgee as were their escorts. When a sparkling point was made, or a clear-cut epigram rang out on the evening air, the dainty-gloved hands were the first to respond, and frequent were the waving of handkerchief and fans.[41]

As stated earlier, most women active in partisan politics lived in urban locales. In contrast, as Paula Baker has recently pointed out, rural women, especially farm women, were usually too burdened with domestic responsibilities to have time for politics in any form. They were also limited by inadequate transportation, a lack of education, and a tradition of male-dominated politics that was stronger than in the cities. Women residing in small towns and villages sometimes belonged to church and charitable organizations, and occasionally they showed some concern for public questions such as temperance. But their interest was difficult to sustain. Women in rural areas, like their urban sisters, were more likely than men to view politics from a moral standpoint—to judge candidates by their character, to evaluate issues as a matter of principle. Motives of friendship and loyalty or of personal economic benefit had less value to them. Although country women were less apt to participate in partisan events than city women, those in small towns did at times take part in campaign processions, or at least cheered male marchers as they watched them parade by.[42]

FORMS OF POLITICAL ACTIVISM

One kind of political ritual that continued to attract female participants of various backgrounds was the flag presentation ceremony. Even though animosities associated with the Civil War era had somewhat diminished, women in many communities still felt motivated to create flags and banners reflecting the ongoing partisan divisions. These items were usually presented to local party leaders (often former military commanders) at a mass meeting near the beginning of the campaign. As was true in the wartime experience, the ceremony frequently included a short speech by the woman chosen to be the presenter. The following report, describing one such Republican meeting in Greenfield, Indiana, in September 1880, is probably typical.

The ladies of our town have shown no little interest in the pending struggle, and last night they showed their loyalty and allegiance to the party that saved the Union by presenting to the Garfield and Porter club a magnificent silk flag. The presentation speech was made by Mrs. Inez Lyon, wife of Captain Stephen Lyon, whose gallant deeds on many fields of battle won for him honor and distinction. Her address was keen, vivid, pointed, and called forth several times rounds of applause. The opening captivated her audience but as she neared the end, raising her voice till every person could hear distinctly, she said: "I place this flag in the hands of Republicans because I know that under their care never a single stripe will fade or a star grow dim." At this the enthusiasm was boundless.[43]

Not only were women attending meetings and other party-sponsored events, but also by the 1880s quite a few of them were being employed as regular campaign speakers. They generally appeared before mixed audiences, and they almost always received widespread approval. Not every state party organization utilized female lecturers, but in New York and Massachusetts, and especially in the Midwest and Far West, they were increasingly in demand. One popular figure on the Democratic side was Lizzie O'Brien Pollock of Brooklyn, who made several noteworthy speeches on behalf of the party's presidential nominee in 1880, Winfield S. Hancock.[44] Among the best received on the Republican side was M. Adele Hazlett of Hillsdale, Michigan. Adele Hazlett grew up in a Democratic family, but early on, it was said, she "saw through Democratic sophistry and became an earnest Republican." From the time of her first appearance on the stump after the war, Hazlett proved to be a very effective speaker, "always making votes for the Republican party, by her facts, her logic, telling hits, and brilliant sarcasm." Her pre-election speech at Lansing, Michigan, in September 1880, to a packed auditorium was frequently interrupted by hearty applause. Four nights later in Grand Rapids, Hazlett again captivated the public with her words and her presence. She held her audience's attention for two hours in "one of the most logical, earnest, eloquent, and convincing speeches of the campaign," declared a reporter present. He concluded by saying the party should use her more often as a campaign speaker.[45]

The frontier state of California seems to have been the one most accepting of women speakers, judging by the number who appeared at campaign meetings there. Perhaps the two most notable performers were Nellie Holbrook Blinn and Clara Shortridge Foltz. Nellie Blinn, a native of the Midwest and one-time schoolteacher, had moved to California and married a former Union officer after the Civil War. She then became a popular stage actress but seems to have found time during election years for a good deal of stump speaking on behalf of the Republican party. A participant in most California election contests from the 1870s through the 1890s, Blinn also spoke elsewhere for the national ticket. She was, in fact, a featured speaker at Cooper Union in New York City inaugurating the 1880 campaign, and she gave several speeches in Indiana that year as well.[46] Iowa-born Clara Foltz, one of the first women to practice law in California, took part in a number of Republican campaigns in the Golden State in the early to mid-1880s. Then, in 1886, she bolted the party to support the Democratic candidate for governor, who, when elected, appointed her as a trustee of the State Normal School. Foltz continued to favor Democratic candidates for a while but was back in the Republican camp by the end of the century. Both Blinn and Foltz were ardent advocates of woman suffrage, and late in her life—at age eighty-one—Foltz ran unsuccessfully in the Republican gubernatorial primary on a women's rights' platform.[47]

Women were not only employed as campaign speakers during these years but also began to be used as precinct workers on the local level. Such women canvassed their districts and served as poll watchers on election day. One such individual was Mary L. Hall, a light-skinned former slave from Georgia, who began working for the Republicans in Savannah in 1869. "The people were voting in the Court House and the polls were open all day long, and when I went out I saw the advantage that the white people were taking of my people, giving the colored voters Democratic tickets and the negro men did not know any better. I saw that I could be of use," she said, in explaining how she got involved in politics. A few years later Hall moved to New York City and was employed at the Customs House, a position she probably received for her continuing efforts in behalf of the Republican party. On one occasion she described for a reporter her vote-seeking activities in the black district on the west side. "I make a room-to-room canvass. I even go into the gambling places and dives where I think colored men are likely to be, and make them come out and register. Then, on election day, I make them vote. This is the dirty work I have done. . . . Every election day I serve soup, coffee, sandwiches and cigars to voters. You cannot get colored men to vote without spending money one way or another." On the morning of the election, Hall was out before the polls opened and stayed there until closing time to watch what transpired, looking to expose members of the opposition who tried to cast illegal ballots. As she had done in Savannah years earlier, she also helped some constituents who had difficulty reading to mark their tickets properly.[48]

Most of the political activism by women described here in the decades after the Civil War took place in the North and West. The postwar South, in contrast, saw female interest in politics decline from what it had been prior to and during the war. As George C. Rable has recently written: "Few any longer bothered to comment on public questions in their letters and diaries, and political discussions apparently became less common in southern homes. If women usually ignored state or local elections, they paid even less attention to national contests. Partisan politics seemed increasingly irrelevant to daily life when the South's future in the Union remained bleak and uncertain."[49] Of course, not all women were completely detached from the political scene. As time passed, some, especially urban white women, attended parades and other campaign events as they had done before. Also, early in the Reconstruction era, as Professor Eric Foner has noted, a number of black women came to political meetings and even wore campaign buttons to promote the candidacy of General Ulysses Grant in the 1868 presidential race.[50] Moreover, northern white women, who went south after the war to educate blacks and help them adjust to freedom, often encouraged the election of Republican candidates among the ex-slaves. Finally, a few native white southern women did participate very actively, and one of them, Rebecca Latimer Felton of Georgia, virtually ran her husband's congressional campaigns and served as his chief administrative assistant in the nation's capital.

North or South, Rebecca Felton was clearly in a class by herself as a campaign coordinator and administrative aide in the latter part of the nineteenth century. She did the work of a whole political staff as manager of her husband's election bids and overseer of his congressional duties in Washington. Felton, a college graduate and one-time schoolteacher, learned about politics during the Civil War, "in front of Gatling guns and Mauser rifles," as she put it. In 1874, when her husband, Dr. William Felton, ran in his first race for Congress as an independent candidate, Mrs. Felton "was in the thick of it." As she later recalled:

Without a daily newspaper, and only two little weeklies that hot canvass was made by Dr. Felton on the stump and my individual work with my pen. I wrote hundreds of letters all over fourteen counties. I wrote night and day, and for two months before the close kept a man and a horse at the door to catch every mail train three miles away. How I lived through that ordeal I never can tell. The like of this campaign was never known before or since in Georgia. At one time [my] health broke down, but I was propped up in bed with pillows and wrote ahead. I made appointments for speaking, planned for speakers, answered newspaper attacks, and more than all kept a brave face to the foe and a smiling face to an almost exhausted candidate. Dr. Felton spoke three times a day on an average, and that meant three fresh shirts a day. But I had those shirts ready when he rushed in, all packed and ready as he rushed out and away into that fearful exhausting struggle.

Naturally, she felt her efforts were all worth it when her husband won the race, albeit by a narrow margin.

Rebecca Felton continued her frantic pace during her husband's three terms in Congress.

I was up and ready for a six years' struggle in and out of Washington where I still wrote letters, wrote for the newspapers for constituents before the departments, doing the work of the present clerks to congressmen, and without expecting a cent, but just for the love of the work and loyalty to Dr. Felton's interests. In some of the campaigns I traveled with him all over the district. In other campaigns I "stayed by the stuff", and planned the campaign. The history of my life during that period would surpass a novel in startling surprises, because the fight of the independent congressman never ceased or abated one iota.

She herself was attacked by opponents for her reform efforts, especially in her role as an advocate of prohibition when she worked for the Women's Christian Temperance Union in her state. Rebecca Felton, in fact, heard herself "denominated as the political 'She' of Georgia." But Felton was not one to back away from her critics. "Whenever they showed [their] heads above the ramparts, this sharpshooter in a woman's form deliberately picked them off for public amusement and feminine revenge."[51] Felton would continue to be involved in Georgia politics for several more decades. She was extremely active in the Populist crusade during the 1890s, and later in 1922 she made political history when, a widow in her eighties, she briefly served in the U.S. Senate, the first woman ever to do so.

Thus, by the late nineteenth century, women were becoming more active in partisan politics, sometimes through the suffrage movement, though mainly through their own personal interest in the ongoing party struggle. Women were now more apt to become partisan speakers and attend mixed gatherings, as well as engage in the forms of electioneering that they had been a part of since before the Civil War, for example, hosting picnics and marching in parades. Some women received appointments to minor public office, and a few even ran for elective positions (though usually without much success). Women were hardly near the centers of power, yet their actions made them clearly more visible than their earlier counterparts.

Chapter 5

Reform Politics and Partisan Activity

As noted in the previous chapter, many more women participated in partisan politics in the post–Civil War period, but they were still acting mainly on the periphery. While Rebecca Felton may have managed her husband's congressional campaigns and worked in Washington, D.C., as his administrative assistant, no woman exercised political authority to any significant extent. A few served as campaign speakers or wrote articles, a few ran for office, and a considerable number did canvassing or received low-level appointive posts. But these as well as the vast majority who simply attended party meetings or marched in parades were essentially supporting players. Ultimately, some women did play a more central role, having entered politics in a different way: joining reform groups and then affiliating with minor parties. Operating within an alternative framework, they were frequently able to exert a greater degree of influence than those associated with the major parties. The effectiveness of these individuals as campaigners soon caused the traditional party leadership to begin employing women on an expanded basis in their organizations as well.

THE TEMPERANCE MOVEMENT

Perhaps those most responsible for initiating this change were the women of the temperance movement. Temperance had long been an issue of deep concern to women, who were often the victims of abusive alcoholics in their families or in society at large. Although antiliquor agitation first appeared before the Civil War, it was in the early 1870s that the temperance crusade really began to flourish. Women in many states started circulating petitions to have liquor outlawed, and they picketed outside saloons seeking to shut them down. When this effort brought just limited results, some of these women came to believe that their ends could be achieved only through direct political action. According to a recent scholar, such organized political efforts occurred in at least sixty-one communities in thirteen states around 1873 and 1874. In many of these instances, women became active in referendum campaigns or attempts to elect sympathetic legislators or city councillors on totally "dry" slates. On these occasions, women sometimes participated in the nomination of candidates, the canvassing of neighborhoods, and, in a few cases, the casting of local ballots. Most of the persons taking part, coming from conservative backgrounds and believing in traditional Christian views about a woman's place, had difficulty moving into this new realm. They often engaged in a great deal of soul searching about whether or not to defy society's standards in this regard. Nevertheless, spurred by the desire to curb the use of alcohol, women's involvement in temperance-related political activities would increase markedly during the next few decades.[1]

The chief vehicle for those opposed to hard drinking in the years after 1874 was the Women's Christian Temperance Union (WCTU). Formed by religious enthusiasts mainly from the Midwest and Northeast, many of whom had been involved in previous antiliquor crusades, the WCTU provided the necessary organizational means to challenge the system, "a sophisticated avenue for political action." Not everyone agreed with this approach, of course. Some of the more conservative members such as Annie Wittenmyer, first president of the Union, believed that the "traditional female methods of persuasion and prayer" were the only appropriate ones to take. But the majority eventually followed Frances Willard, a former schoolteacher from Illinois, who firmly advocated using direct political means. A charismatic and dominating figure, Willard became WCTU president in 1879 and remained in charge of the organization until her death in 1898. (By that time the WCTU's national membership had grown to almost 170,000.) Willard, in addition to opposing liquor, was also deeply interested in advancing women's rights and saw the temperance movement as providing an important step in that direction. Even before she took over the WCTU leadership, she was pushing for a limited form of woman suffrage known as the Home Protection ballot. Under this proposal, women would get the right to vote in local-option elections, where questions of saloon licensing and outright prohibition were being considered.[2]

Support for political action within the movement encouraged Willard, two years after she became WCTU president, to adopt a "Do-Everything policy" at the organization's national convention in 1881. This plan allowed state and local groups to pursue a wide range of options in attacking "demon rum." It declared that "wisdom dictates the Do-every-thing policy: constitutional amendment, where the way is open for it; Home Protection where Home Protection is the strongest rallying cry; Equal franchise, where the votes of women joined to those of men can alone give stability to temperance legislation." The most controversial aspect of "Do-Everything" to many of the group's members was the endorsement of woman suffrage. Although a few of them chose to resign from the WCTU in response to this move, the majority supported it, allowing those who wished to do so to engage in suffrage as well as temperance work. Like Willard, most of the rank-and-file came to see that only through the ballot could they have a chance to accomplish their main goal. The WCTU's involvement in suffrage activity not only brought it into closer contact with the political system, but it also set the stage for a virtual linkage with the Prohibition party.[3]

Prior to this time, when it came to political preferences, most WCTU members (in the North at least) nominally favored the Republican party. The Republicans, after all, had been the party that preserved the Union, freed the slaves, and seemed to be more seriously concerned with moral issues than the Democrats. Republicans in many locales were advocates of temperance, and in 1880 GOP presidential candidate James Garfield had made a pledge to support the temperance cause. However, when the new Republican administration showed little interest in following through on this matter, the WCTU leaders started to look elsewhere and subsequently moved toward an alliance with the dozen-year-old Prohibition party. The Prohibitionist organization had been created in 1869 by members of a religious group—the Good Templars—in upstate New York. From the beginning the party accepted women members—thirty were delegates to its first convention—and endorsed woman suffrage. Over the years, the Prohibitionists had displayed little overall electoral strength at the national level, but on the state level it had taken away enough votes to bring about the Republicans' defeat in a number of instances.[4] In the long run, the Prohibitionists hoped to use this power as a lever to force the Republicans to fully embrace their point of view.

ALLIANCE WITH THE PROHIBITIONISTS

An alliance with the Prohibitionists was not easy for the WCTU to accomplish. As stated above, many WCTU members wished to remain loyal to the Republicans, which in certain states took a strong antiliquor position. But Frances Willard and numerous other leaders recognized the opportunities to be gained by the new connection. They quickly organized an affiliate group—the Home Protection party—which in 1882 merged with the Prohibitionists. At Willard's insistence, the new association was to be called the Prohibition Home Protection party so as to affirm women's stake in the temperance movement and to maximize WCTU support. Actually, the national WCTU board, containing a number of staunch Republicans, had not endorsed Willard's moves, and at the group's annual convention that fall it forced Willard to accept a compromise. It was resolved that in the future the women should "influence the best men in all communities to commit themselves to that party, by whatever name called, that shall give to them the best embodiment of prohibition principles, and will most surely protect our homes." Nevertheless, this did not stop the drift toward an alignment with the Prohibitionists since in many communities they were the only party taking a strong stand on the alcohol issue.[5]

During the 1884 national election, after being rebuffed again by the Republicans on the temperance question, Frances Willard and some of her close associates agreed to play a major role in Prohibition party affairs. They were seated on the main platform throughout the party convention and made significant addresses to the delegates; Willard herself delivered the chief nominating speech for the party presidential candidate John St. John, former governor of Kansas. Unlike the exclusively male conventions of the major parties, the Prohibitionist gatherings reflected strong feminine influence: "Not a taint of tobacco smoke was in the corridors; not a breath betrayed the fumes of alcohol."[6] Although the Prohibitionists, even with active WCTU support, generated less than 1.5 percent of the popular vote nationally that year, the alliance between the two continued. In 1888, of the roughly 1,000 delegates attending the Prohibition party convention in Indianapolis, about 100 were members of the "steadfast sex," and WCTU officials once more took a leading part. Both Willard and temperance orator Mary Lathrap of Michigan presented major addresses. Willard also served on the resolutions committee regarding woman suffrage. She and other prominent figures like Helen Gougar of Indiana made campaign appearances in many states and virtually gave over the WCTU newspaper to the promotion of the party effort. As Ruth Bordin has written, "The columns of the *Union Signal* read like campaign tracts that summer and fall. In a single issue seven and a half columns were devoted to an enthusiastic account of the Prohibition party convention, and there was also a two-column biography of its presidential candidate [former Union general Clinton B. Fisk]."[7]

Fisk and other male Prohibition leaders praised the female contribution to the party and exhorted women to do everything in their power to further the cause. "As a woman's inspiration depicted the great wrong of slavery, till men could endure the hideous sight no longer, but swept it away, so in the fight against this gigantic evil we know that the ballots cast for its destruction will many of them come first through women's hands," declared Fisk on one occasion.[8] Early in the campaign, one Massachusetts spokesman, Robert Pittman, told the temperance women of his state: "You are an integral part of the Prohibition party. This is your cause as well as ours; nay, more so, for it touches the home most closely, and the home, which is the solace of man, is the world of women. . . . We look to you in hope as our reserve corps, who at the last will make our victory overwhelming and final. Meantime you can be effective allies. No great uplift of humanity was ever made without enthusiasm. Of that woman's heart can be the fountain. Women can aid in much of our practical work; and if it cannot put a vote into the ballot box it can be stretched forth in eloquent appeal to those who have deprived her of self-protection to be manly enough to drop the shackles of old party ties and stand themselves for protection of the home."[9]

Although female temperance advocates played a major role in the 1888 Prohibitionist campaign, their contribution, as was the case four years earlier, brought meager results. The party was resoundingly defeated on the national level, getting only 2.2 percent of the total vote. Indeed, after the election, the WCTU began severing its attachment to the Prohibitionists, finally realizing the link had done little to limit liquor use or bring about woman suffrage. Some WCTU members resumed ties with the Republicans, although Willard thought that such an alliance would offer nothing better since both of the above-mentioned issues would be virtually ignored by them. By the early 1890s, Willard, still wishing to make gains through a political connection, started exploring a possible alignment with the newly formed People's or Populist party. The Populists' advocacy of many egalitarian economic reforms attracted Willard, who had become deeply influenced by Edward Bellamy's utopian socialist novel *Looking Backward* (1887). She saw the Populists putting together a broad coalition of farmers and laborers, which, she felt, might be sympathetic to both prohibition and woman suffrage. Willard met with Populist leaders

Ignatius Donnelly and James Weaver, hoping to work out an acceptable reform program. But the Populist convention in St. Louis in 1892, showing caution as it launched its first national campaign, could not accept inclusion of a strong prohibition plank in its platform; nor could it agree on a pro-suffrage plank either. Although as individuals some temperance advocates chose to support the Populist cause in the general election that year, it was impossible for the WCTU as a group, given its main reason for being, to take such a stance.

In the years following 1892, the WCTU would play a less active role in national politics, and it gradually moved away from any direct party involvement. The failure to reap much benefit from the previous decade's partisan attachment and the desire to curb internal division within the organization surely prompted this change. Some individual members of the WCTU continued to take part in the campaigns of the Prohibitionists, but the Union itself never again endorsed the Prohibition party by name. At the WCTU convention in 1894 it did agree to offer "prayers and influence to any party which puts Prohibition and Equal Suffrage in its platform." It also commended the state parties in the West which had taken a strong temperance stand. Yet that was as far as the leadership would go. Indeed, after 1896 there was not even a hint of a political endorsement from the WCTU convention, and following Willard's death in 1898, the Union started shifting over the next decade toward a position in line with the nonpartisan, single-issue Anti-Saloon League.[10]

THE POPULIST MOVEMENT

While numerous women in the post–Civil War era drifted into politics in the quest for temperance, some middle-class reformers as well as individuals in the working class did so through one of the small parties connected with organized labor. This process began in the late 1860s, when Susan B. Anthony and Elizabeth Cady Stanton, in their desire to promote equal suffrage, had sought to build a network of close allies in the labor movement. Although a strong alliance ultimately failed to take shape, quite a few suffragists and female union members became associated with the Labor Reform party, the political arm of the National Labor Union, in the early 1870s. Greater numbers of women subsequently got involved when this labor group joined forces with the more broadly based Greenback party later in the decade. (The Greenbackers took a pro-labor position but also appealed to the farming community, especially in its advocacy of "soft money" as an economic panacea.) Few sources ever mention women engaging in specific partisan activities for the Greenback party or its successor in the mid-1880s, the Union Labor party. Nevertheless, an open letter by one female thus affiliated during the election campaign of 1884 claimed that contrary to the indifferent stance toward women taken by the major parties, they were welcome in its ranks. Indeed, several notable women in the subsequent Populist struggle got their political start in one of these farmer-labor organizations.[11]

Some farm women, especially in the South and West, would enter the political world through a related group, the Farmers' Alliance. The Alliance had become a significant advocacy organization in the 1880s and 1890s, seeking to improve conditions for farm families in the rapidly changing, increasingly industrial society of the time. Members hoped to gain favorable legislation in the states in order to combat monopolies, regulate railroads, and raise farm prices. Like the earlier farm protest group known as the Grange, the Farmers' Alliance in most states accepted women on an equal footing and welcomed their participation. "Equal rights to all, special privileges to none," was their slogan. Ultimately, one-third to one-half of the membership was made up of women. Within the Alliance, women were encouraged to gain an education and become more adept in helping their family's farm to prosper. At its regular gatherings, women had an opportunity to discuss major economic, political, and social questions, "to try out ways of behaving in mixed groups, and to gain confidence in newly acquired skills." Indeed, for many women, being in the Alliance offered them their first chance to act in any way political—to write letters to the press, speak in public, and hold offices. Naturally, they found themselves facing certain limitations. No woman was ever named president of any local chapter, and the stated goals of the Farmers' Alliance never included women's political rights. Nevertheless, a number of individuals, especially from the Plains states, did wield considerable influence in the Alliance and in the subsequent Populist movement.[12]

One of these women was Luna E. Kellie of Nebraska. Kellie, who had been a farmer's wife and mother of eleven children in the postwar period, had no political background to begin with. But seeing the widespread poverty around her and the inability of the existing system to cope with the problem, she eventually thought it necessary "to resort to politics to get any needed reform." First active locally in Kearney County, Kellie served as secretary for the Nebraska statewide Alliance, helping to arrange lectures and other events for several years. In addition, she edited and distributed a Populist newspaper from her home.[13] Another woman who contributed her pen and also her voice to the movement was Sarah Emery of Michigan. Emery, who had earlier been active in the Greenback and Union Labor parties, became a leading writer and lecturer for the Farmers'

Alliance/Populist cause by the late 1880s. Emery's widely distributed books *Seven Financial Conspiracies* (1888) and *Imperialism in America* (1892), which sharply attacked the financial power of Wall Street bankers, helped her become a highly coveted speaker at Populist conclaves for several years, until her premature death in 1895.[14]

One of the foremost figures in the creation of the Populist party on the national level was Annie Diggs of Kansas. An economic reformer, temperance advocate, and religious "free thinker," Diggs first joined the movement as the associate editor of an Alliance newspaper in the town of Lawrence in the late 1880s. After working with the People's party in the Kansas statewide election of 1890, she started lobbying for a national third party at various Alliance conventions during the next couple of years, and she was a major force at the Omaha convention launching the People's (Populist) party nationally in 1892. Her power in the party, especially behind the scenes, would continue to expand right up to the time of the organization's demise around 1900. On the state level throughout the 1890s, Annie Diggs was often successful in creating "fusion" tickets, giving Populists a chance to hold certain high offices in the Kansas government. It also caused opponents to raise the complaint of "petticoat domination" by "Boss" Diggs.[15]

Among the women thrust into politics through the Farmers' Alliance and Populist movement none would make as great an impression as Mary Elizabeth Lease. Born and raised in the East before emigrating to Kansas in 1873, Lease taught school for a while, then married a pharmacist, had four children, studied law, and passed the bar. Lease formally entered the political arena in 1888, when she spoke at the state convention of the Union Labor party in Wichita, calling for reforms to aid the farmer and laborer. During the People's party campaign in Kansas in 1890, she delivered over 160 speeches and claimed responsibility for the defeat of longtime Republican senator John J. Ingalls. Lease, nearly six feet tall with a rich and powerful speaking voice, became the most notable Populist orator—male or female—in the 1892 presidential contest. Drawing big crowds on the stump in several states, she urged farmers to "raise less corn and more hell." When the People's party took power in Kansas in 1893, Lease was appointed president of the State Board of Charities. However, because of her outspoken and uncompromising nature, she proved unable to get along with party regulars and was subsequently ousted from her post. In fact, Lease often did better as an agitator than as an officeholder. Continuing conflict with the party leaders ultimately led her to sever her Populist connections, and, curiously, she wound up supporting the Republicans in 1900. In later years, Lease remained politically active and used her talents at times as an advocate of woman suffrage. But in that and subsequent endeavors, she never regained the prominence she had achieved during her association with the Populists in the 1890s.[16]

Populist women in the southern states played a less significant political role than did those in the western (Plains) states. Southern men were less inclined to allow women to hold office, make policy, or deliver public speeches, and few women ever did. (Indeed, Mary Lease was sometimes treated harshly by crowds when she spoke in the South during the 1892 presidential campaign.) Nevertheless, southern male Populists understood that women had comprised a considerable part of the Farmers' Alliance in their section, and knew that they could influence the vote of husbands, brothers, sons, and other male relatives. Therefore, Populist leaders made sure to invite women to rallies—even black women sometimes attended— and often called on them to perform certain politically related chores. Generally, women responded with as much zeal as the men, even though the "politically related chores" consisted mainly of arranging picnics and similar events. Yet if members of the female sex did not usually obtain positions involving major responsibilities, there were always some exceptions. In Georgia, for example, the clerk at the state Populist headquarters was a woman. In addition, Lulu Pearce, an associate of party leader Tom Watson, served as secretary and bookkeeper of the *People's Party Paper*, the movement's main newspaper in that state. Although their actions were not always very visible, women's contributions to the Populist cause cannot be discounted.[17]

The influence of women in the Populist movement is reflected in the party's open espousal, after 1892, of woman suffrage, a reversal of its initial position. Of course, this policy change was due not only to pressure from women in the organization like Lease but also to the growing belief that the party would gain support, particularly in the West, if it adopted a pro-suffrage stance. In a number of western states, the Populists soon made suffrage a central issue, and in Colorado, where a Populist governor and majority in the legislature had been elected, they succeeded in giving women the ballot in 1893. Populists in the legislature had backed the bill 22 to 3, while Republicans and Democrats had opposed it 24 to 12. When the referendum was submitted to the voters statewide, it was the Populist-leaning counties that provided the margin of victory. (Ironically, the Populist governor in Colorado then lost his reelection bid in 1894 partly because the state's newly eligible female voters did not rally to his support in sufficient numbers.)[18] The Populists also became the first party to favor woman suffrage in Idaho. While eventually all parties in the state endorsed the reform and had a suffrage resolution placed before the electorate in 1896, it was the Populists who had done the most to achieve this goal.[19]

THE SOCIALIST PARTY

After the fall of Populism at the end of the century, a number of women in that and other reform movements would be attracted to the new Socialist party founded in 1901. (Some female reformers, including the late Frances Willard, had already been converted to the doctrines of Christian or Bellamy Socialism.) These women were attracted not only by the socialist vision of a better, more enlightened, and more egalitarian world, but also by a seemingly greater offer for them to participate in the reordering and rebuilding process than in other political organizations. Women, in fact, would make up 10 to 15 percent of the early Socialist party membership. One woman who would exemplify the shift from Christian reformer to Socialist agitator was Kate Richards O'Hare, who grew up on a farm in Kansas and then did religious and temperance work in Kansas City before joining the socialist cause. Besides those of this background, a considerable number of women in the socialist camp were European born and well versed in Marxism; they had come to socialism through the women's labor movement. A key figure was Theresa Malkiel, who emigrated from Russia in the 1890s and had organized the Woman's Infant Cloak Makers Union. Malkiel believed workers needed political as well as economic organization, and therefore, she helped promote the Socialist party. Important socialist women in subsequent decades included the New York–born, Irish-American orator Elizabeth Gurley Flynn, and Meta Berger, wife and political associate of Victor Berger, who for many years was the socialist mayor of Milwaukee.[20]

The Socialist party was pledged to sexual equality and always included support of woman suffrage in its party platform. Yet that and other female issues did not have a high priority among the male leaders, who saw women mainly as a component in the proletariat that would help overthrow capitalism. In fact, probably a majority of men in the movement fully believed in the old order when it came to gender roles. Nevertheless, wishing to bring more recruits of both sexes into the socialist fold, they agreed to establish a woman's section of the party and give its members some authority. Like other politically active women, those in the Socialist party attended rallies, marched in parades, and handed out literature during election campaigns. However, unlike the auxiliaries attached to other parties, many socialist women had greater interest in organizing labor groups and promoting strikes than in electoral activities. In addition, as time passed, some of them began to devote increasing energy to various aspects of the "woman question," for example, equal rights, birth control, and sexuality, rather than sticking simply to economic matters. Ultimately, this fragmentation of concerns would weaken women's contribution to the Socialist party, and indeed weaken the party.[21]

MAJOR PARTY ACTIVITIES

As women proved effective in promoting the fortunes of third-party movements, the major parties showed a greater willingness to employ them as well. Although no concrete evidence connects the Republican and Democratic responses to the minor parties' actions, it is perhaps more than a coincidence that their initial moves occurred at roughly the same juncture—the late 1880s and the early 1890s. The men in charge of the major parties must have observed the damage being caused by third-party female auxiliaries, and understood the benefits that such campaigners could bring to their own operations. The year 1888 was the turning point as they recruited many more women and employed them in a wider variety of vote-getting activities than had been the case in previous elections. The change was noted by temperance advocate Frances Willard, who among other things described how "women escorted speakers, paraded in foot processions, and in several instances occupied the ancient and honorable place always heretofore accorded to the brass band."[22] In Chicago, for example, a Young Ladies' Republican Marching Club, with an initial membership of fifty, regularly appeared at party events. Women lecturers were also more conspicuous than before. Even the celebrated Anna Dickinson, absent from the hustings for many years, agreed to give a series of speeches for the Republicans in the Midwest to counter the influence of the Prohibitionists and their female speaking contingent.[23]

J. ELLEN FOSTER AND THE WNRA

A development of deeper importance that year than the wider range of female electioneering was the huge proliferation of partisan women's clubs. Such groups had existed in small numbers in previous decades but now came to be organized on a broader and more formal basis. Local Republican clubs were often called "Carrie Harrison clubs," after the wife of the GOP presidential nominee Benjamin Harrison, whereas Democratic women's clubs invoked the name of Frances Cleveland, the young wife of Grover Cleveland, the incumbent president. The Republicans would make more systematic use of such clubs, and before the campaign was long underway, created a central body, the Women's National Republican Association, to coordinate these clubs' activities. The WNRA was headed by lawyer and temperance advocate J. Ellen Foster of Iowa; indeed, the move toward forming the umbrella organization may well have been Foster's idea. Foster, who had recently split away from Frances Willard and the Women's Christian Temperance Union because of their Prohibitionist party ties, turned out to be a superb politician and organizer. Largely through her efforts, nearly 1,000 local chapters of the WNRA were established by the time of her death in 1910. The group initially consisted of a small executive committee—president, secretary, and publicity director, plus 300 field workers. But the membership would grow to many times that figure over the next two decades. Beginning in 1892, the WNRA had its own official publication, *Home and Flag*, which in its first issue laid out the association's objectives: to organize Republican women into local associations, to hold frequent meetings to study and discuss Republican doctrines, to circulate partisan literature and contribute items to local newspapers, to influence first-time voters, and to cooperate with regular (male) GOP organizations in doing party work.[24]

Foster herself was extremely effective as a campaign coordinator in her more than two decades of service to the party. Putting to use the experience she gained in the temperance movement, Foster supervised several door-to-door canvasses in which she strongly brought to bear the female influence on the male vote. In 1892, she masterminded the Republican vote-getting operation in parts of New York City; in 1894, she led the successful attempt to oust the Populist governor of Colorado, and in subsequent elections applied her methods in other western states, where women had acquired the vote. Foster, though not a woman suffrage leader, sympathized with the suffragists' goal and spoke in favor of a constitutional amendment before GOP platform committees at various state and national conventions. She also continued to advocate temperance on those occasions. But Foster was a practical politician and never let her support for suffrage or temperance interfere with her Republican commitments. "We are straight out-and-out Republicans and stand on the Republican platform," she told a leading suffragist in 1888. Regarding the vote, Foster believed that over time women working for the party would tend to convince others "that they need the ballot." She also thought that through their deeds female activists would help gain the respect of male politicians who could eventually bring about equal suffrage.[25] For her enormous contribution, she and her husband would be generously rewarded with government appointments over the years. In addition, Foster's loyalty and dedication enabled her to gain entrance into high party circles.

Indeed, she was about the only woman included in the top-level strategy sessions of the Republican National Committee during this period.

A contemporary account of the Foster-led campaign effort in New York City in 1892 demonstrates the thoroughness of her methods and the unique ways in which women sought to obtain votes. Together with close ally Helen Varick Boswell, secretary of the WNRA, J. Ellen Foster in lower Manhattan launched

a tenement house canvass which still stands as a classic example of women's party work. Miss Boswell had headquarters on Broadway, and sixty women helpers. Daily they swept down upon the foreign East side taking it block by block, house by house and—as was necessary in the congested parts—literally room by room. While mothers rocked cradles with their feet and with their hands sewed buttons onto shirts, the women talked to them of school, street cleaning, and health protection. When younger women came home fagged from their day in the department store or the factory, the canvassers met them with party promises concerning labor.

In addition, brief, simple pamphlets in all languages were put into the hands of children, who might read them to their parents.

So, a man coming home at night, slightly fuddled with promises and a cheap cigar, the souvenirs of a street corner harangue by a ward heeler for the opposition, would walk into a united family who also had promises, but instead of cigars, had reasons. He was indeed an egoist if he did not change his mind. As a matter of fact he generally did change his mind, as was shown on election day. Wards went Republican that had returned big Tammany majorities for a quarter of a century.[26]

In smaller communities, Foster and her Republican association often had to compete for women's allegiance with the temperance movement and the Prohibition party. As a longtime opponent of alcohol use and a former member of the WCTU, Foster understood that many women were interested in establishing restrictions on drinking, but she warned them against seeking total prohibition or joining the Prohibition party. Total prohibition, she felt, was an unrealistic goal, and the Prohibition party was a politically hopeless organization, operating against women's best interests. The Prohibitionists, she asserted, took advantage of women, using them for their own narrow purposes, flattering them with worthless honors. "[I]t gives women seats in conventions, and places their names on meaningless committees and tickets impossible of success. . . . The pity of it is that women, gentle and refined, and sometimes strong, should be

vain enough to be thus cajoled and their God given powers thus mort-
gaged."[27] Foster believed that if women wanted to achieve a total ban on
liquor, they needed to change public attitudes on the subject. Only such
laws that follow public opinion could work successfully, she added. The
Republican party with its moderate antiliquor position presumably took
the best approach for her.

If Ellen Foster operated most of the time as a modern, practical politician, the message she delivered to potential Republican recruits often
contained some traditional sentiments about women—that they were
different from men and had a different role to play in politics. Yet at the
same time her words foreshadowed the argument that reformers would
stress throughout the Progressive period, namely, that women should use
their greater moral sensitivity to help clean up corruption in government.
These views can be observed in an address Foster made to a convention
of Republican women in Buffalo, New York, at the outset of the 1892
presidential contest. After some preliminary remarks about the kinds of
campaign work that women could expect to perform, she focused on her
main theme: how women could purify politics. Foster said "it was an
acknowledged fact that the influence of women was great and why should
it not be in politics, in pure politics, as in other pure things? The relation
of women to politics would be to purify them, to make issues moral ones,
and to educate at least their sons, the voters, to vote for their country's
welfare, and not simply in a blind way, for a party."[28] Foster encouraged
women to study Republican doctrines and assumed they would see that
the GOP had the highest level of integrity. Speaking on the same subject
to a women's gathering several years later, Foster admitted that the
Republicans were not all saints nor the Democrats all sinners. But, she
added, there was good reason to support the Republicans rather than the
Democrats. "I believe that the principles and policies of the Republicans
are *righteous*, that they are an interpretation of the spirit of the Constitution
as well as its letter."[29]

Helen Varick Boswell, Foster's close WNRA associate and founder of
the West End Republican Association in New York City, at one meeting
spoke even more closely to traditional female interests when appealing for
women's help at election time. "I think that all women should favor the
Republican party because it is the party of the home. From the home all
good things spring," she asserted, and the issues before the country should
be discussed between wives and husbands in the home. But Boswell also
stressed the idea of the Republicans as the party of economic prosperity.
"Under the rule of the Republicans," she said, "the prosperity of the
country has been assured and all home industries are protected." She

added that one of the main reasons for her allegiance was that she was a businesswoman and the Republican party was "the only party that knows how to conduct an administration on business principles."[30] On another occasion, when she and some colleagues attended a predominantly male campaign luncheon, Boswell facetiously but probably not inaccurately showed a no less important side to female support for the GOP. "I suppose . . . you men will want to know first why we are Republicans— and I'll tell you. It's because we love good clothes, good things to eat, nice furnishings in our homes. Then too, we don't like our husbands to be cross and look worried as they did when the Democrats were in power."[31]

THE ELECTION OF 1896

During the critical election of 1896—"the battle of the standards"— between William McKinley and William Jennings Bryan, Republican women, indeed women of many stripes, became deeply involved in the contest. "In no year since the civil war," it was widely agreed, "had women taken so general an interest in politics as this year." In practically every state, women were attending political rallies and "doing quiet and effective work for the parties and candidates of their choice."[32] Even black women were active in McKinley's behalf, with the reformer Ida Wells-Barnett leading the way in Chicago. Noting the "exceptional interest in the campaign" by its female readers, the *Boston Herald*, a Republican newspaper, prepared a series of special articles for their consumption. Naturally, J. Ellen Foster and her associates were active in mobilizing local women's Republican clubs and giving speeches in several western states, particularly Kansas. To counter the Populist arguments of the late Sarah Emery in her widely read pamphlet on "Financial Conspiracies," Mary F. Henderson, the wife of a former Republican senator from Missouri, penned what became a highly influential tract, "The Issue of the Campaign—Sound Money," which the national committee circulated in huge quantities.[33] Women's contribution to McKinley's victory was so well recognized by party officials that prior to the next congressional contest in 1898, the Women's National Republican Association was for the first time given a separate headquarters in Washington, D.C., from which to carry on their future electioneering activities.[34]

Although male Republican leaders clearly understood the female contribution to the party cause, it did not bring them any closer to granting women equal political rights. Indeed, the party platforms between 1880 and 1892 contained no mention of the subject whatsoever.

In 1888, the platform did say that it recognized "the supreme and sovereign right of every lawful citizen to cast one free ballot in all public elections," but this was not construed to include women citizens. In 1896, the platform committee, after listening to an impassioned appeal by pro-suffrage spokesmen, did adopt the following plank, which held out some hope. "The Republican party," it stated, "is mindful of the rights and interests of women. Protection of American industries includes equal opportunities, equal pay for equal work, and protection to the home. We favor the admission of women to wider spheres of usefulness, and welcome their co-operation in rescuing the country from Democratic mismanagement and Populist misrule."[35] Yet this statement, with its seeming commitment to improve women's condition, did not precipitate any political reforms once the Republicans were elected. The Democratic party never mentioned women in any of its platforms during this period, and the Populists, who had shown some support for woman suffrage in the early to mid-1890s, did not press the issue when their party fused with the Democratic organization in the election of 1896.

DEMOCRATIC WOMEN'S ACTIVISM

Although the Democrats made no reference to women's rights in their platforms and did less to encourage women's involvement in politics on any level than the Republicans, this did not mean that all Democratic women were inactive or indifferent. In 1892 Mrs. Virginia D. Young of Fairfax, South Carolina, a Democrat like most white southerners of the post–Reconstruction era, claimed that women in her vicinity were often the strongest partisans. "I am sure," she said, "I cannot recall a gubernatorial election when the women of our State did not take sides, hear discussions, throw flowers to the speakers, and indicate their partisanship in every possible way." For presidential campaigns too, they were "as pronounced in taking sides as men," and they flocked to see candidate Grover Cleveland when he toured the area.[36] In that same year, Democratic women in the northern states had created numerous local partisan clubs, which were affiliated nationally as the Frances Cleveland Influence Club. Their goals were "to voice woman's interest in campaigns of principle; to defend the homes of the land against unjust taxation; to secure the election of the Democratic ticket."[37] When Cleveland and his wife objected to the use of Mrs. Cleveland's name in the title, it was changed to the Democratic Influence Club. During the next two national elections (1896 and 1900), the Democratic women's organization would be called the Women's National Bryan League in honor of the party's presidential nominee, and thereafter it was known as the Women's National Democratic Club. In the Bryan campaigns especially, Democratic women took upon themselves a considerable part of the canvassing.

Outside the Northeast, probably more women were attracted to the candidacy of William Jennings Bryan than to any previous presidential aspirant. Few presidential nominees before him had such charismatic appeal, and few had ever turned regular political issues into great moral questions. His crusade-like effort had its strongest impact in the trans-Mississippi West—the region where women had already been fairly active politically. So it did not take much prodding to get them—if they were not committed Republicans—to host events, distribute literature, and otherwise aid in Bryan's quest for election. Some even gave speeches or wrote pamphlets on the silver question, the campaign's central issue. One group very useful in this regard was the Women's National Silver League, an auxiliary of the National Silver party, which sponsored public forums promoting the free coinage of silver as the best means to solve the nation's economic woes.[38] The enthusiasm for Bryan's candidacy in 1896 can be seen in a letter from Caro Lloyd Withington, the sister of Henry Demarest Lloyd, muckraking author of *Wealth Against Commonwealth*, toward the end of the race. "We illuminated [our house] last evening for the Bryan local parade, and we hung Grandpa Lloyd's enormous big flag with 26 stars. I couldn't resist putting 'Bryan and Sewell' on the edge of our little flag to help on the cause." Withington added that she felt terribly disappointed that she could not do more for Bryan's election, such as vote.[39]

Interestingly, Bryan's most valuable supporter in 1896, as well as in all his other campaigns, was, in fact, a woman: his wife Mary, a practicing attorney. Bryan's leading biographer describes her role in the famous contest in these words: "His chief aide and counselor in the campaign was not some seasoned politico or facile expert in public relations. It was Mary who usually traveled with him, coached him and advised him on his speeches, and oversaw the endless tons of correspondence. Mary helped conserve Bryan's strength by meeting reception committees at the succession of railroad stops, thus permitting her husband more rest between speeches. And Mary was shrewd in her estimates of political people who came into Bryan's presence."[40] One contemporary wrote that "the speech in Congress which first brought Mr. Bryan into national prominence was written by his wife, [and if he wins] she will bring an intellectual character . . . even perhaps a salon [to the White House and will] compel women to think about the issues of the day."[41] After the defeats of 1896 and 1900, the Bryans continued their political partnership through a periodical called *The Commoner*, in which they spoke out on a number of causes. Yet not until 1915 did Bryan, like other leading Democrats, commit himself publicly to woman suffrage.

With many women aiding Bryan and the Democratic ticket in the late nineteenth century, some Republican editors used the situation to strengthen the argument against equal suffrage. Even though Bryan lost the election of 1896 by a sizable margin, these editors railed about the fact that women in the western states had given him strong backing. Particularly galling to them was the majority Bryan received from female voters in the few states where they had become eligible. An editorial in the *Boston Herald* remarked: "The participation of women in the political affairs of our country does not appear to have been productive of the best results, when judged by the outcome of the last election. In this late contest, in which, more than any other we have had for the last quarter of a century, a moral issue was presented, those States in which suffrage was granted to women threw their vote, without exception, on what is considered the immoral side of the question."[42] A similar view was expressed in the *Philadelphia Times*, which declared that "the association of woman suffrage with Bryanism is likely to give level-headed women pause." It also claimed that the removal of the sexual qualification everywhere would simply "swell the ignorant and cranky vote at least equally with if not in greater proportion than the intelligent vote."[43] Statements of the latter kind appeared before and after other elections around this time, making the first women voters feel that they were on trial regarding their performance at the polls.

In any case, by the end of the nineteenth century women were clearly becoming a greater factor in partisan politics. Their increasingly elevated position in minor parties undoubtedly caused the major parties to start employing women in a more systematic fashion than before. Most significantly, the parties promoted the organization of women's clubs on a wide scale to assist in all kinds of campaigns. Nonetheless, most women in these groups still occupied auxiliary posts and were generally unable to exert much influence over policy and the nomination of candidates. Only in a few western states at the very end of the century would women begin to have some degree of real power as they acquired the right to vote.

Chapter 6

Women Begin to Vote

In the long run, nothing encouraged the movement of greater numbers of women into partisan politics than their being able to vote. Indeed, the noteworthy performance of female voters in the first few suffrage states in the late nineteenth century and after helped break down barriers so that women could eventually cast ballots in all states. Their positive response ultimately put to rest opposition claims that only "low" women like prostitutes would come to the polls, that the women's tally would simply duplicate the men's, and that most women had no interest in politics. In fact, women in the initial suffrage states often showed a political sophistication beyond that of their nonvoting sisters. They were much more likely to join partisan clubs and discuss important issues. As a group, they probably exhibited a stronger preference for political and social reform than women elsewhere. Furthermore, their accomplishments may have influenced reform-minded women in some of the eastern and midwestern states to get involved in the partisan realm even if lacking the vote. Clearly, the actions of these politicized women in the early suffrage states provided models for others of their sex to follow in the years to come.

VOTING IN SCHOOL ELECTIONS

Of course, some female voting in America had occurred even before the western suffrage states were established. As noted earlier, a few unmarried property-owning women cast ballots in colonial times, and a somewhat larger number did so in post-Revolutionary New Jersey (1776–1807). In addition, many women gained partial suffrage rights beginning in the middle decades of the nineteenth century. Despite the almost universal opposition to a full and equal vote for women, some states appeared willing to grant them a limited franchise, specifically in the realm of school board elections. To many people of both sexes, "school suffrage" constituted a proper reform since the education of children was increasingly seen as a woman's responsibility. In fact, the state of Kentucky had offered this option to "widows with children of school age" as early as 1838. The new state of Kansas, when it entered the Union in 1861, gave all adult women the right to vote in school elections. This precedent was followed by five states in the 1870s: Michigan and Minnesota in 1875, New Hampshire and Oregon in 1878, and Massachusetts in 1879. Another nine states, including New York, introduced similar legislation in the 1880s. In most cases, not many women—sometimes less than 5 percent—exercised their newly gained voting rights on a regular basis.[1] Not surprisingly, opponents of equal suffrage used the low turnout rate to argue that most women did not really want the vote. But advocates proclaimed that school elections failed to provide a good test since they were rarely competitive, and when a contest did occur, the totals could climb considerably.

School election returns from the city of Boston in the late nineteenth century attest to this pattern of high fluctuation. Boston women started voting for the school board in 1879, but over the next five years fewer than 700 on average (1 percent) went to the polls. There was usually a consensus regarding the choice of board members during that time. Nevertheless, the numbers showed an increase in the mid- to late 1880s, partly owing to the rise of partisan pressures. Republican leaders, upset at the Democratic-controlled school board's catering to local liquor interests—closing down a school rather than an adjacent saloon—decided to take action. They proposed a highly competitive opposing slate for the next school board election with two women on it. The growing conflict caused both parties to step up registration efforts and to get women to hand in ballots. As a result, the vote more than doubled between 1884 and 1885. The biggest outpouring of all took place in 1888 when the Republicans schemed to win every seat on the board and the Democrats did everything they could to stop them. Almost 17,000 female voters—11,000 on the GOP side, 6,000 on the Democratic side—came out for that year's contest. (Interestingly, this higher figure still represented no more than one-fifth of the potential women voters and only about 26 percent of the male total, which stood near 64,000.) The tally started to fall in the next few elections as a

Table 1
Women's School Vote, Boston, 1879–1903

Year	Number of Votes	Year	Number of Votes
1879	934	1890	7,880
1880	770	1897	5,721
1881	640	1898	5,201
1882	498	1899	7,090
1883	650	1900	9,542
1884	1,026	1901	11,620
1885	2,238	1902	11,819
1888	16,947	1903	13,655

well-organized Republican female club, known as the Independent Women Voters, moved in to dominate the selection process and competition waned. However, as the figures in Table 1 indicate, the turnout level edged upward again in the late 1890s and early 1900s, when new issues began confronting Boston's women voters.[2]

VOTING IN MUNICIPAL ELECTIONS

While women in sixteen states were eligible to take part in school elections by the late 1880s, the state of Kansas went further, yielding to the female demand for full participation in all local elections starting in 1887. According to contemporary reports, the women of Kansas fully appreciated their newly acquired municipal voting rights and went to the ballot box in an eager fashion. At the capital city of Topeka in April 1889, women were said to have displayed more enthusiasm than the men and in some cases even provided the means for those without transportation to get to the polls. A few affluent ladies "sent their carriages to remote parts of the city and brought in numbers of their less happily circumstanced sisters, who needed but the one incentive of rapid transit to make them good nineteenth-century Kansas citizens." Among those descending upon the polling places were "hundreds of colored women," many of whom, it was claimed, "electioneered with all the art of practiced politicians." The female voting process was not without some of the unsavory acts that usually accompanied male voting. In one incident, an illiterate black woman, who wished to vote a straight Republican ticket, was instead given a ballot for the Democratic side by three white women in an alley way. Yet, on the whole, there did not appear to be any significant rise in illegal behavior.

In Topeka, a partition separated the men from the women as they cast their ballots. The women apparently "seemed more impressed with the responsibility of their act" and scrutinized their tickets carefully before passing them through the windows. Many scratched out names from the prepared list and made changes that were visible to the officials present. During the day, several instances of husband and wife voting for different parties occurred, refuting the charge that women were totally under men's influence. Much to the chagrin of the Republicans, a majority of the white women that year supported the Democratic mayoral candidate in Topeka as well as in Atchison and Leavenworth. In the town of Leavenworth, Colonel Dan Anthony, younger brother of Susan B. Anthony, headed the Republican ticket, but even with the help of his famous sister he was defeated by 700 votes. One reporter wondered whether Miss Anthony still favored woman suffrage in Kansas after this contest. (Dan Anthony would eventually be elected mayor of Leavenworth at a later date.)[3]

In regard to how many women voted in the early municipal elections in Kansas, it is impossible to calculate exact percentages owing to the absence of full and accurate census data. However, aggregate figures show that 28,587 women cast ballots in the first year (1887) but just 15,228 in the second year (1888), when only minor offices were to be filled, although the amount rose to approximately 40,000 in the third year (1889), when major positions were contested once more. In Topeka, the totals on those occasions were 1,049 in 1887, 854 in 1888, and 2,479 in 1889. Ten years after municipal suffrage was granted to them, the women of Kansas continued to be responsive, according to fragmentary returns published in the *Woman's Journal*. In Wichita, for example, 2,300 out of 2,327 female registrants went to the polls in 1897, and in 1903, a Republican primary in that city drew 5,943 men and 5,379 women. By the time Kansas women obtained full suffrage rights a decade later, it was estimated that roughly 60 to 70 percent were already regular voters.[4]

The law that allowed Kansas women to vote also enabled them to run for municipal office. This led almost immediately to the designation of a number of women as mayors and many more as town or city council members. The first woman to win a mayorship was Susanna Madera Salter from the small town of Argonia in Sumner County, in the south-central part of the state in 1887. But Salter seems to have been involved in little decision making and was overshadowed in her position by an all-male town council. More notable that year was the election of an all-female town council in Syracuse in Hamilton County in the far southwestern part of the state. Two years earlier, there had been no more than a handful of women in Syracuse. But the town began shifting away from its "Wild

West" stage, and many "good women" moved in and encouraged the building of schools and churches. The newcomers also formed church ladies' aid societies and pressed for municipal reforms. Unhappy with the ticket for the city election headed by newspaper editor H. N. Lester, these women in conjunction with mayoral candidate N. E. Wheeler nominated an all-female council slate. Thanks to the support of the new female voters, the all-female slate won. Once in office, they instituted so many positive changes that even the defeated candidate Lester agreed Syracuse had become "renowned as a city of good government, good morals, fine streets."[5] None of the "city mothers" ran for reelection the following year, but their male successors continued to emphasize the need for municipal improvements and clean government.

Another Kansas town, Okaloosa, went even further than Syracuse, electing both a woman mayor and an all-female council in 1888. These six women, led by Mary Lowman, wife of a prominent businessman, had agreed to run when it became evident that an alternative slate was necessary to counter the lackluster incumbent administration, which had few accomplishments to its credit and had left only 85 cents in the town treasury. All six were politically concerned women determined to improve local conditions. Elected with the aid of their husbands by a three-to-one majority, the "petticoat government" proceeded to clean up the town, enforce the blue laws against alcohol use, widen some of the main streets, and restore funds to the treasury. Their efforts also brought them reelection and national notoriety. But the all-female contingent did not become permanent. In what seems to have been a pattern in several places, the women did not remain in office very long once the reforms had been instituted. Nevertheless, the success of these women encouraged the nomination of other female candidates seeking local posts in the state. For example, in 1889, the small towns of Cottonwood Falls and Rossville placed the entire government in the hands of women, as did Jamestown in 1897. By the end of the century, fifteen women had been named mayors of Kansas towns, and many dozens more chosen to serve on town councils.[6]

THE FIRST FULL SUFFRAGE STATES

Kansas males refused to allow female voting beyond the municipal level, defeating a statewide referendum in 1894 to extend it further. Yet, by 1896 women had acquired full suffrage rights in four other western states—Wyoming, Utah, Colorado, and Idaho. Wyoming and Utah had first given women the vote more than a quarter of a century earlier when

both were fledgling territories. The Democratic-dominated territorial legislature of Wyoming, partly to advertise the region to potential settlers and
partly to embarrass the appointed Republican governor, had approved
woman suffrage in late 1869. Early the next year, the Mormon-controlled
legislature of the Utah territory followed suit. The action of the Utah
leadership was undertaken mainly to counter accusations that Mormon
women were virtual slaves and also to hasten the path to statehood. Two
decades later, suffrage for women in Wyoming was reaffirmed with its
advancement to statehood in 1890, the new constitution specifically
permitting adult females to take part in the election process. In contrast,
Congress withdrew woman suffrage in Utah in 1887 in an attempt to
punish the practitioners of polygamy. However, when Utah became a state
in 1896 (with polygamy officially outlawed), the franchise for women was
reinstated. Suffrage advocates in Colorado and Idaho had a tougher
internal struggle to obtain their goal. But, as mentioned earlier, thanks to
the efforts of the Populists and other pro-suffrage groups, women's right
to vote was achieved by referendum shortly after each of these territories
acquired statehood: Colorado in 1893, Idaho in 1896.[7]

In these four equal suffrage states, it is clear that a high percentage of
women frequently exercised their voting privileges and took part in
partisan politics in other ways as well. In Wyoming, where women had
been voters since territorial elections began, one end-of-the-century
spokesman said that they used the franchise "at first not very generally
but of late with universality, and with such good judgement and modesty
as to command it to the men of all parties."[8] By 1900, it was estimated
that up to 90 percent of the women eligible to vote did so regularly, about
the same level as for men. Although few women in the state ever held
high elective office (no female legislator was chosen before the twentieth
century), a number served in low-level appointive positions. Many
others were active in their respective parties, canvassing their districts
at election time. Yet, for some unexplained reasons, women in Wyoming
generally played a less conspicuous role in politics than those in the other
three full suffrage states.[9]

In Idaho, where equal suffrage was approved by a large majority in 1896
and went into effect in 1897, the women's vote immediately became an
important factor in shaping local results. In Boise's first municipal election, most women backed the mayoral ticket which favored a wide range
of public improvements, and that side won by a larger plurality than had
been predicted. In addition, women got elected to the posts of city collector
and city clerk. The initial statewide election where women voters were
permitted (1898) saw a heavy turnout, with the female rate of participation

as high as the male. Women cast approximately 40 percent of all ballots at a time when they comprised about 40 percent of the population. Three women were chosen to the legislature—one Republican, one Democrat, one Populist—four were selected as county treasurers, and fifteen as county superintendents of public instruction. Moreover, the state superintendent of schools designated that year was also a woman. The turnout of Idaho's female voters diminished somewhat in 1900; women supplied over 40 percent in the more urban parts of the state but only 35.5 percent of the overall total.[10]

In Utah, right after the territorial government was established in 1870, many women began taking a "practical interest in public matters." They served as delegates to conventions and as members of territorial and city commissions. Yet no woman could hold major office until statehood and a new constitution received approval in 1896. From that time on, however, women were chosen to several state positions such as county auditor, treasurer, and recorder, and in the first election three ran successfully for the legislature. Two made it to the lower house and one—Martha Hughes Cannon—to the upper chamber. Women managed to be elevated to high posts in both major parties too. In 1896, Mrs. Emmeline Wells, who was also a leading suffragist, was named vice-chairman of the Republican State Central Committee, and another woman, Julia Farnsworth, got appointed as secretary. In addition, women played a big part in local and statewide campaigns. During the heated contest of 1896, for example, "the ladies of Utah," according to the *Salt Lake Tribune*, "did first-rate work. They organized their clubs, they spoke in various meetings; they were as earnest in enthusiasm for their cause as the men." As far as voting was concerned, Utah women were said to have been no less diligent than their male counterparts. Although no exact figures are available for the 1896 election, it would seem that the participation rate among eligible voters was about 80 percent for each sex. Four years later in 1900, 28,486 of the 29,732 registered women cast ballots.[11]

The extent of women's involvement in partisan politics at this time is best documented for the state of Colorado. A contemporary field study by a well-trained social scientist, Helen Sumner, examining the first dozen years of voting by Colorado women (1894–1906), not only provides figures on the level of turnout but also gives a thorough analysis of women's overall political role in the state. As was true in other western locales, female voting ran almost as high as male levels, and perhaps even higher in the initial stages. Although working with incomplete data, Sumner estimated that about 47 to 48 percent of the total ballots before 1900 were cast by women, when they comprised less than 42 percent of the population. In 1900 itself, women furnished 41.5 percent of the votes in the presidential election, less than 1 percent under their statewide proportion. For 1904, Sumner's tally of several precincts in Pueblo County revealed women furnishing 46 percent of the total in the more urbanized areas, though only 25 percent in highly rural areas, where they were fewer in number. Her survey of returns from nine counties in the state election of 1906 disclosed that women then comprised 47.4 percent of the population, 41.5 percent of the registered voters, but only 37.3 percent of the actual voters.[12]

As to voting behavior, Sumner found that women in the better residential districts in Denver and Pueblo voted more frequently than women from poorer districts, that single women participated more than married women or widows, and that Mexican-American women went to the polls less often than Mexican-American men. In terms of candidate choice, she observed that women more often than men acted independently and seemed less likely to be influenced by partisan considerations. This can be seen in the precipitous rise of split-ticket voting once women acquired the franchise. Women were deeply concerned about the personal character of the candidates and tended to have a positive effect on the caliber of men chosen to stand for office. Saloon keepers and men of questionable morals were rarely nominated any more. This was particularly true in the mining towns. As one resident described the shift: "Before equal suffrage this mining camp was governed almost wholly by the saloon element. Now it is almost impossible to elect a saloon man to office."[13]

In regard to the gender of officeholders, no great movement arose through the parties or otherwise encouraging women to seek most major or even minor posts. As Sumner pointed out: "There is some unwillingness manifested by men toward allowing women to be nominated for any political office except for state and county superintendent of schools and for certain offices in small towns where the salary is no object."[14] The old attitude still prevailed that men were needed in top positions and that paying jobs should by rights go to men, who normally supported women in the home. However, women did manage to get appointed in a few cases as county clerks, auditors, or assessors, and in much greater numbers to various state boards, which handled health and welfare matters. For example, on the Board of Charities and Corrections, the figure rose from seven to seventeen in the first year following the suffrage law. In fact, the tally of women on all state boards went from 140 in 1894 to 185 in 1906.[15]

Despite the prevailing belief that only men should fill high elective positions (and indeed they won every seat in the upper house), ten women got elected to the lower house of the legislature in the first decade of equal suffrage. Although no more than two or three received the nod in any year, it still must be considered a major achievement. In terms of background, all ten of the women were either married or widowed, several having grown children. Most of them had been club women of some prominence in their local community. According to Sumner, the record of these women in their legislative capacity was "fair, but not brilliant. . . . In the number of committees on which they served, of resolutions which they have offered, and of bills which they have introduced, they have averaged as high as the men." But as legislators their small numbers put them at a major disadvantage. As one male politician pointed out: "They are ineffective because they do not attend caucuses, etc., where the real work is done. They don't attend these because they are not asked. They simply go to the floor and vote. There would have to be more of them to have any real influence."[16]

In one phase of political work, however, women did achieve high marks. When it came to canvassing, a majority of women and 35 percent of men Sumner surveyed said that women were more efficient than men. (Only 16 percent of the men she polled saw women as less efficient canvassers.) As one Denver matron described the situation: "The women are more thorough. Men hurry through." And a Boulder resident added: "[Women] are really better, for they love to get into a house that they have never been in and find out all they can, political and otherwise."[17] In the larger communities of the state, women undertook most of the campaign canvassing, although this was much less the case in smaller rural locations. Another area of women's political effectiveness was in getting out the vote on election day. Women often volunteered to do housework and watch children so that a mother could go out to vote. Sometimes women also provided the means of transportation—carriages and automobiles—to those of either sex who were otherwise unable to get to the polls. Furthermore, women in many instances served as poll watchers for their party to make sure the voting ran smoothly.[18] All in all, their contribution to Colorado politics was a major one.

The phenomenon of women voting in Colorado and three other western states prompted a careful examination of their political performance and intensified debate over whether the vote should be extended to women elsewhere. Both pro-suffragists and anti-suffragists claimed that the results reinforced their particular view, although sometimes the evidence was exaggerated. Supporters of woman suffrage in Oregon, for example, issued a pamphlet pointing out that in the states where women voted the population had increased, and manufacturing and agriculture had grown, without mentioning other factors involved in the region's development. On the opposite side, critics of suffrage like former president Grover Cleveland declared that women's impact on the politics of the four suffrage states was "neither elevating nor refining."[19] Anti-suffrage spokesmen focused especially on the Mormon influence in the West, asserting that the addition of female voters only strengthened a political minority that was "not only un-American regarding our governmental ideas but anti-American." Overall, it would be fair to say, as did one neutral observer, that the presence of women in the political arena "neither unsexed her nor regenerated the world."[20] However, it was hard to deny that after women started voting in the western states, the cities had better sanitation and the quality of the schools improved. Also, politically, the level of moral character among candidates for office was raised, and a more refined atmosphere around the polling place became evident.

Regardless of whether commentators saw their participation as positive or negative, women voters had become an increasingly important factor in the outcome of national and state races by the turn of the century. This was borne out by the appearance of more and more male candidates addressing female groups during campaigns and the growth of appeals to women in the states where they possessed the franchise. It can also be observed in the numbers of women joining partisan political clubs and taking part in pre-election festivities. In 1900, the Women's Democratic Club of Colorado claimed a membership of 10,000, while the Women's Republican League in that state probably stood at an even higher figure. Members of both clubs worked very hard for their respective tickets that year. Indeed, according to an article in the *Denver Republican* that October, "never had women taken such a lively interest in politics."[21] At the beginning of the presidential campaign of 1904, major newspapers around the country carried a feature story entitled "Woman Factor in West," which noted how the Republicans were going to expand electioneering efforts among women in the four suffrage states, especially since the number of female voters might reach 100,000. The author of the article argued that the four western states—containing fourteen electoral votes—were all in the doubtful category and that the women of those states might for the first time be the deciding factor in electing the president of the United States, the Republican Theodore Roosevelt, or the Democrat Alton B. Parker.[22]

Interestingly, the outcome in three of the states in 1904, Utah, Wyoming, and Idaho, seemed to hinge on the issue of Mormonism, which had direct implications for women. The Mormons had developed a close alliance with the Republican party in the election four years earlier, and this alliance was now being heavily criticized by leading Democrats in those states. These men managed to get an anti-Mormon plank adopted into each state's party platform and to nominate anti-Mormon candidates on their state tickets. Led by Senator Fredrick T. Dubois of Idaho and former Senator Frank Cannon of Utah, the Democrats made a special appeal to the women voters of the region, telling them to forget their party affiliations and come out for the anti-Mormon side. The Republicans became so concerned about the situation that they sent J. Ellen Foster to the scene to try to combat the Democratic moves. Whether it was due to the efforts of Mrs. Foster or to the overwhelming popularity of Theodore Roosevelt in the West, Roosevelt won every electoral vote in each of the above-mentioned states. However, the majority of non-Mormon women did go against the Republicans in Utah and, in addition, helped elect a Democratic mayor in Cheyenne, Wyoming. In Cheyenne, it was said, women had always displayed a great deal of independence on local issues.[23]

Not only in the West but also in the Midwest and the East, where women still could not vote for any state or national offices, their participation in campaigns was on the rise by the turn of the century. During the national election of 1900, according to one female observer, suffragists and anti-suffragists alike were "donning McKinley and Bryan badges" and "joining McKinley and Bryan Leagues."[24] Even students at many women's colleges were involved. Everywhere, it seemed, women canvassers were leaving few stones unturned in their effort to influence the results, trying to "ensnare the vacillating voter at his workshop, his home and his pub." "From West to East," wrote one reporter that same year, "Their voices are heard and their methods are recognized."[25] One young woman in Minnesota named Eloise Calihan was even put in charge of campaign scheduling by the Republicans for the entire state. She operated with a staff of over one hundred men and women under her command, and went about arranging times and places for scores of events, transportation to and from obscure country towns where those events were to occur, and a host of other details. Miss Calihan, according to her associates, was "a born politician" and had "a masculine ability to size up the situation that is phenomenal."[26]

In political races around this time, as the historians Richard Jensen and Michael McGerr have pointed out, the major parties began adopting new patterns and forms of electioneering. The spectacular campaigns of the post–Civil War era featuring torchlight parades and brass bands were giving way to a more dispassionate educational style—emphasizing informative speeches and the distribution of massive amounts of literature discussing important issues. This style was most evident in the

Republican response in 1896, managed by McKinley's friend and associate, businessman Mark Hanna, to Bryan's "free silver" crusade. In the ensuing years, the new format would also come to include merchandising techniques designed to sell the candidates through "slogans, simple messages, . . . magazine advertisements, billboards, phonograph records, and films." Women campaigners may have influenced the adoption of these new methods, and indeed feminine assistance was sought in preparing many of the innovative materials described. Yet some of the old ways of vote-getting persisted. Campaigns still contained ceremonial events, speakers, and rallies, and a great deal of canvassing still went on at the local level. It was in canvassing that women became a vital force, going into the immigrant neighborhoods, eventually helping to make municipal reform possible through the ballot box.[27]

WOMEN'S ROLE IN MUNICIPAL REFORM

If women were exerting some influence in state and national campaigns around the turn of the century, they probably had their greatest impact on the outcome of municipal elections in the growing metropolises of the East and Midwest. Even before that time, women had been engaging in numerous kinds of urban reform activity. Inspired by crusading social workers such as Jane Addams and Florence Kelley, women's reform groups in various cities pushed for improvements in factory conditions, a ban on child labor, as well as better schools and housing. They also worked for safer streets, cleaner water, more effective garbage disposal, and other forms of sanitation. To obtain their goals, women reformers operated through municipal leagues and city clubs. These organizations held meetings and put out literature to publicize their causes. In addition, they lobbied at city hall and in the state legislature. Because these efforts did not always bring about the desired changes, some members (though by no means all) started to engage in partisan politics. In doing so they ignored critics who claimed they would lose their independence and objectivity if they became politically involved in this manner.[28]

One vigorous effort to bring about municipal reform by political means involved Jane Addams herself. Addams's famed settlement known as Hull House lay in Chicago's Nineteenth Ward, which in the 1890s was controlled by a corrupt and powerful boss named Johnny Powers. Addams blamed Powers for many local ills, particularly for doing little about widespread neighborhood filth and disease, as well as for failing to support the building of a new public school in the ward. In the first of three electoral battles with the machine, in 1895, Addams encouraged the Hull House

Men's Club to run an independent candidate against Powers' henchman for the post of alderman. Although the independent triumphed, he was soon bribed so heavily by Powers as to become his most loyal ally. Addams then went after Powers himself. In 1896 she personally masterminded the campaign against the boss, bringing in outside speakers, bombarding local residents with handbills, and in general making reelection more difficult for the well-entrenched incumbent. On election day, Addams and her Hull House followers succeeded in cutting into Powers' usual voter margin, but Powers still won. Once again in 1898, Addams and friends sought to oust Powers from his position as ward boss, writing essays and organizing residents into various ad hoc clubs. Powers struck back hard this time, claiming Hull House and its head were anti-Catholic and anti-immigrant. Posters denounced the female participation in the campaign as the coming of "petticoat government," and Addams was harshly condemned for entering politics in the first place. Although Powers was victorious by a bigger total and not directly challenged again, Addams and the other women involved had publicized municipal problems, gained political experience, and perhaps influenced women elsewhere to take up similar causes.[29]

A greater foray by women into the partisan municipal realm can be seen in the city of New York. At that time New York City government was under the control of the notorious Tammany Hall machine. While local Tammany chieftains did provide certain benefits to the poor and heavily immigrant population, massive corruption by Tammany-backed officials drained huge amounts of public money from necessary city services and allowed vice operations—such as gambling and prostitution—to proliferate. Many women, upset by this situation, had long championed reform and joined various groups aimed at cleaning up government, but not until the mid-1890s did they begin to take part in anti-Tammany election campaigns. After making a limited appearance in the mayoral contest of 1894, women's presence was particularly strong in behalf of independent candidate Seth Low in the mayoralty race of 1897. Answering the call of longtime reformer Josephine Shaw Lowell, head of the Women's Municipal League, to take action in order to "protect the life and morals of their children by securing honest government," many women engaged in house-to-house canvassing and distributing literature. They went especially to the "foreign districts" of the city to spread their message and try to register voters.[30] Recently formed female Republican groups such as the West End Women's Republican Association also played a very active part in the latter phase, allying themselves in the effort to bring down the Tammany machine.

Yet despite the contribution of these reform-minded independent and Republican women, Seth Low was defeated as the male Republican leadership rejected a fusion ticket and ran their own candidate, which split the anti-Tammany vote. Nonetheless, the heavy turnout for Low showed many people the positive effect of employing female campaigners.[31]

In fact, their participation in the 1897 contest caused many men to reverse previously held negative views about women's involvement in partisan politics. Certain civic leaders such as the influential minister Lyman Abbot, who had formerly insisted that women should not take part in politics because they could not spare the time to inform themselves on public questions, now began to praise their campaign work. Early in the race, the editor of the popular magazine *Outlook* sought to impress on women the idea that they could not make safe and healthy homes merely "by keeping everything spotless within their four walls if the city is materially and morally foul around them."[32] Most ironic of all was the response of the pro-Tammany Democratic newspaper to the phenomenon of Republican women forming clubs and working in the campaign while Democratic women remained inactive. In a sharply worded editorial, it asked: "WHERE ARE THE DEMOCRATIC WOMEN?" Chiding the pro-Tammany ladies for their indifference to the big issues at hand, the writer declared:

For every Democratic voter in New York there is at least one Democratic woman. In everything but the mere casting of an individual vote a woman may count for as much in politics as a man. For the next six weeks political work will be a matter of influence, argument and industry. In all these respects there need be no distinction of sex in the usefulness of believers in Democratic principles. Let us have some Democratic Women's Clubs.[33]

Although some female workers could be found on the Democratic side in 1897, the response was limited partly because such women tended to be from less educated and affluent backgrounds than their anti-Tammany counterparts. In any case, the majority of those active in that contest and other local races of the next two decades continued to be arrayed in behalf of independent candidates or Republican-led fusion tickets against the entrenched Tammany machine. In 1901, Republican women and members of organizations such as the Women's Municipal League and the Woman's League for Political Education were again crucial elements in a coalition that finally elected reform candidate Seth Low as mayor. Working together with male reformers from the nonpartisan City Club, the women in the campaign raised several thousand dollars, which was very useful in supporting their canvassing and publicity efforts. They also printed an influential pamphlet, "Facts for Fathers and Mothers," which described children's involvement in the prostitution racket, a leading issue in the contest. J. W. Pryor, secretary of the City Club and coordinator of the women's activities in the last stages of the race, claimed that "the women had done more campaign work than had ever been accomplished before in New York in the same length of time."[34]

A few months later, Oswald Garrison Villard, one of the era's leading reformers, summed up the contributions of women to recent political campaigns in New York City and how public attitudes had changed toward women in politics. "Twenty-five years ago," he said, "such a thing as a woman's headquarters, distributing pamphlets, raising money, getting up meetings, supplying speakers, and furnishing one of the most effective arguments of the entire campaign, would have aroused a storm of indignation and scorn, and would have evoked endless announcements that the fatal hour, so often prophesied," which would mark the unsexing or "masculinization" of women was at hand. When women participated in the municipal campaigns of the early 1890s, there were even then "not a few protests and publicly uttered regrets that women should concern themselves with the political conditions of the city." In 1897, while women's assistance was heartily welcomed by the reform candidates, "they were still regarded as curiosities and their actions were reported by the public press much as the illustrated Sunday newspapers today portray things freakish, passing and unusual the world over." However, by the end of that campaign, women's substantial contribution was beginning to be recognized. Finally, in the aftermath of the election of 1901, said Villard, it was clear to almost everyone that women had been one of the strongest factors in the reform ticket's success.[35]

Women continued to play a very active role in the New York City mayoralty races of 1903 and 1905. By 1903, membership in the Women's Municipal League had risen to about 250, and these along with many other women worked hard, trying to keep Seth Low in office. The league formed a thirty-one-member campaign committee to coordinate activities in the city's various districts. Women who could speak any of the languages of the major immigrant groups toiled long hours in the district offices, preparing and distributing literature, and counseling immigrant men on how to register. Women also delivered speeches on moral issues—male reformers often felt that moral rhetoric would have greater weight coming from women. Yet all the female campaigners' endeavors were not enough to bring about Low's reelection. Somehow, the Tammany machine had improved its image and made the reform ticket with its emphasis on government by trained experts look like a party of aristocrats. Mention of "fashionable ladies" promoting the reform slate probably had a negative effect on some male voters too. In 1905, the Tammany mayoralty candidate was reelected, but organizations like the Women's Municipal League did help elect reformer William T. Jerome as district attorney. After 1905, women reformers began focusing more on the study of serious urban problems—housing, school, health care, and so on—and less on electing particular candidates. But local partisan groups like the West End Women's Republican Association kept their attention centered on electoral campaigns and continued to provide major assistance to their party.[36]

Around this time, female influence also played a prominent part in the election of reform candidates in Philadelphia. In 1905, women in the "City of Brotherly Love" eagerly answered the call to help clean up the corruption in the municipal government, which had long been under the control of the notorious Durham organization or "Gang." Operating under the slogan, "This is not politics, but morals," a women's committee of the new reformist "City Party" was organized. They began distributing literature and arranging meetings in nearly all of the city's forty-two wards, where they could address the neighborhood's female residents. Among those taking part were the mayor's sister-in-law and Mrs. Owen Wister, wife of the western novelist. They and others often spoke before two or three women's groups daily. The main theme in their speeches and their printed materials was always the same—the best means of safeguarding the home consisted of vigilant effort outside the home against those forces trying to subvert it. "Housekeepers, attention," exclaimed one pamphlet, do you want good government in Philadelphia? Then it listed the evils of the existing system—graft, protected vice, assessment of public salaries, police corruption, tax increases, and "other things bad for you." "If these are some of the results of government by the 'Gang,' why should they do any better now? Why trust them any longer? What is your duty? Urge every man you can to vote for the City Party ticket." Undoubtedly, the women's message got through, for partly through their participation, the "Gang" was defeated, and the reformers were elected by a 43,000 majority.[37]

WOMEN AS PROGRESSIVES

Beyond the municipal level, women reformers took part in many congressional and statewide political campaigns on behalf of progressive candidates. In the state of Wisconsin, for example, they helped elect Robert M. LaFollette to the governorship and worked to keep him in office, supporting his many progressive reforms. LaFollette later wrote in his autobiography: "In all my campaigns in Wisconsin, I had been much impressed with the fact that women were as keenly interested as men in the questions of railroad taxation, reasonable transportation charges, direct primaries and indeed the whole progressive program."[38] In fact, by 1912 when the progressive forces had created a national party, they had given women major places of responsibility, even seats on the national committee. As one Progressive party publicist later remarked: "Woman has been welcomed, both as auditor and speaker. She has been taken into party councils, and has been given a position of leadership in no degree less prominent than that of men. Her presence and the promise of her larger participation in the duties of citizenship and of government have been greeted with greater enthusiasm than any other phase of the movement."[39]

Naturally, many reform-minded women were deeply involved in the Progressive party campaign of 1912 seeking to elect Theodore Roosevelt to the presidency. Women were among the delegates to the inaugural Progressive convention and helped design the party platform. This platform, with its commitment not only to equal suffrage but also to many kinds of social welfare reform—including restrictions on child labor, minimum wage legislation, and old age insurance—was especially attractive to women. In addition, officials of major women's organizations and leading social workers such as Jane Addams were placed on the party's highest councils. Addams herself gave one of the chief nominating speeches—the first woman to do so for a major candidate—and devoted much time and energy to the campaign. All around the country, women were quick to join Progressive Leagues and Bull Moose Clubs to work for Roosevelt's election. In those clubs, women received a greater proportion of offices (from one-third to one-half) and engaged in more speechmaking, fund raising, and literature distribution than had ever been the case before. Women were even running for some statewide offices. So strong was women's commitment that a writer in the *Chicago Tribune* stated: "This is the first time in local history that women have identified themselves so intimately with the political aspirations of any one organization."[40]

Two women of special interest in the Progressive campaign of 1912 were Ruth Hanna McCormick and Frances Kellor. McCormick, the daughter of Mark Hanna, the famous Republican party manager of the McKinley era, had been deeply involved in politics from an early age. At age eighteen she had become her father's chief secretary when he was chosen to the Senate in 1898. After marrying Medill McCormick in 1903, she became active in several reform causes in Chicago, and in 1912 she joined her husband in promoting Theodore Roosevelt's candidacy, serving as a leading member of the Progressive party's campaign committee. Over the next three decades, she would continue to play an important role in politics, including a successful run for the House of Representatives and an unsuccessful run for the Senate.

Whatever her position, McCormick thoroughly enjoyed the game of politics, as did Frances Kellor. Kellor, who attended Cornell and studied social work, had earlier in the century been a busy reformer in New York, heading commissions investigating the living conditions of recent immigrants. The effectiveness of her work had drawn the attention of President Roosevelt, who subsequently appointed her national director of publicity and research when he mounted his campaign in 1912. From her position, Kellor promoted woman suffrage and sought to convince women that, in contrast to other parties, the Progressives offered them a unique opportunity to find a national voice. Unlike many suffragists of the time, Kellor had no qualms about getting involved in "the mean business of politics."[41]

A progressive-minded woman who played a major role on the Democratic side in 1912 was Florence "Daisy" Harriman. Brought up among the upper classes in New York and married to J. Borden Harriman, son of the railroad tycoon, Daisy, like others of her background, developed an interest in certain reforms. She also gravitated toward partisan politics and became an enthusiastic supporter of Woodrow Wilson, agreeing to head the Women's National Wilson and Marshall Association to help elect the Democratic ticket. In that office, Daisy Harriman organized women's groups in a number of cities, engaged in fund raising, and gave many speeches during the campaign. The following year, she promoted the reform candidacy of John P. Mitchel in the New York City mayoralty race. Along with other female activists, she felt for the moment that "woman's place was on the soap box." She and her coworkers employed some very innovative techniques to attract listeners. "We hired wagons, had them backed up to the curb at various downtown locations, and at noon when the canyoned streets ran black with voters, we motored from cart-forum to cart-forum and made our speeches to bank clerks and to . . . longshoremen." After the victory, Mrs. Harriman helped Mitchel make appointments to his staff and was also called to work in Washington for the Wilson administration on certain commissions.[42]

Another woman of the same class who became politically active around this time on the Democratic side was Eleanor Roosevelt. Coming from a political family and having listened to the conversations of her uncle Theodore from an early age, she was already politically knowledgeable when her husband Franklin entered public life in 1910 after being elected to the New York State legislature. Looking for something to do beyond managing a household or being a society matron, Eleanor became active in her husband's behalf, dealing with his colleagues and his constituents, discussing issues and other matters of interest to them, and sometimes acting as a go-between. As Blanche Cook has written in her recent biography: "FDR listened profoundly to his political wife as he listened to few others. It was she who went around and found out what his colleagues and their wives really thought. She went out among his constituents and talked with them, she attended Senate and Assembly debates regularly, and she reported on the subtleties and tricks lodged in every issue."[43] Certainly, Eleanor Roosevelt's behavior was not at all common for the time. But it was by no means unique either, and she probably influenced some of her female contemporaries to do some of the same things.

WOMEN'S VOTING TURNOUT IN THE PREWAR YEARS

During the dozen years or so before American entrance into the First World War, the percentage turnout for women voters remained fairly high both in the older suffrage states and in the new ones added after 1910. In the four original suffrage states, the proportion ranged from 72 to 90 percent, according to actual figures as well as estimates by high-level officials. Wyoming's governor in 1905 reported that 80 to 90 percent of women regularly voted and that 90 percent had taken part in the most recent election the previous year. Utah and Idaho officials gave 75 to 85 percent as the general estimate in their states. In Idaho, 76 percent of women handed in ballots in 1912, only 8 percent below the level for men. "The large vote cast by women," declared the Idaho secretary of state, "establishes the fact that they take a lively interest." Women's totals in Colorado were only slightly lower—75 to 80 percent on average. Female registration in that state reached 80 percent in 1908, and 72 percent of eligible women actually voted in the national election that November.[44]

California and Washington, both of which allowed women to vote by 1911, also experienced turnouts that were quite high. For Washington, an estimated 85 to 90 percent of women came forth the first time they were eligible. Locally, women cast about one-third of the total vote—22,000 out of about 70,000—in Seattle that year for the recall of "corrupt" mayor Hiram C. Gill. Women participated heavily in the recall vote of the mayor and city commissioners of Tacoma as well. California women exhibited even greater zeal to go to the polls once they received the vote. According to one contemporary, never in American history had there been such a rush of new registrants. In Los Angeles, a huge number of women hastened to place their names on the rolls, and over 80 percent of those registered actually cast ballots in 1912, when they became eligible. Mayoralty contests the following year (1913) also drew large female turnouts in several locales. In a state where men still predominated by a ratio of 4:3, Berkeley and San Francisco women cast 46.6 percent and 34.5 percent of the total in their cities' respective mayoralty races. An overall study of returns from 37 of the state's 58 counties in 1913 showed that almost half the women voted and that 61.3 percent of the registered women actually handed in ballots compared to 56.4 percent of the registered men.[45]

Looking at some of the other western states such as Oregon, Kansas, Arizona, Nevada, and Montana, which all permitted full female suffrage after 1912, we note that the figures again indicate a substantial number of votes by women, although no exact breakdown of the overall totals was ever made. In Oregon, where men outnumbered women by about three to two, 137,040 votes were cast by men in 1912, whereas 248,052 were cast by both sexes in the 1914 gubernatorial race and 261,650 in the 1916 presidential race. In Kansas, the election of 1914, which was the first there with full enfranchisement of women, saw an increase in the total vote in almost the exact same proportion as the addition of female voters. For Arizona, the secretary of state reported that the percentage of women voting in the gubernatorial race of 1914, which was also the initial one under equal suffrage, was probably higher than the percentage of men who had voted in the prior male-only contest (1912). In Nevada, with twice as many men as women, almost 33,000 voted in the first equal suffrage election (1916) compared to 20,000 in the two previous state races, 1912 and 1914. Montana's female turnout in 1916 was proportionately even higher than Nevada's, for the total vote was almost double the all-male levels of 1912 and 1914. Montana women that year also demonstrated their political clout by helping to send three of their gender to the state legislature.[46]

Voting by women in the second decade of the twentieth century was recorded separately only in Illinois, the first midwestern state to move toward equal suffrage. (Illinois had granted women the vote in presidential elections and also permitted municipal suffrage starting in 1913.) The results show a much wider gap in male-female differentials than in the several western states where women had been voting earlier. In the presidential contest in 1916, 54.2 percent of the eligible women took part compared to 79.6 percent of the eligible men, a 25.4 percent differential. In the Chicago mayoralty election of 1915, approximately 44 percent of the women cast ballots along with 73 percent of the men—a

29 percent differential. However, the Chicago women did demonstrate an element of independence, having voted in the Republican primary in higher numbers for the "good government" candidate than for the man designated by the party machine. But in other races what we now call a gender gap was not too prevalent. Normally, just a few percentage points separated the male and female tally for each name on the ticket. Overall, the newly enfranchised women behaved like any other newly enfranchised group—lower levels of registration as well as a smaller degree of partisan attachment. Foreign-born women participated less frequently than those who were native-born. Moreover, as might have been expected, women went to the polls more frequently for the major contests—involving the choice of high-level officials—than for minor ones and were less likely to complete a full ballot containing referendum material. Nevertheless, women showed more interest than men in voting on moral questions such as prohibition.[47]

Although the state of Illinois alone provides exact figures on women voting in these years, a few contemporary studies attempted to indirectly calculate turnout (not always very successfully) or at least provide an analysis of women's stance on major issues. In the area of women's positions on the issues, William Ogburn and Inez Goltra, two political scientists from Oregon, a recently added suffrage state, looked at women's preferences in the election of 1914 in the city of Portland, where a number of initiatives and referenda were on the ballot. Although the statistical techniques and categories they used are somewhat questionable, especially the designation of precincts as "radical" and "conservative," it seems apparent that a clear correlation did exist on certain issues. More female than male voters opposed eight-hour work day restrictions for women and several other governmental reforms. On the other hand, far more women than men favored the prohibition of alcohol, as well as the disfranchising of noncitizen immigrants, who in Oregon had been allowed to vote for president. While unable to measure gender differences for the next presidential election, Ogburn and Goltra imply that the women of Portland identified more strongly with the Republicans, even though Oregon as a whole went Democratic in that contest.[48]

Whatever the analysts might have said about their performance at the polls, women by the eve of the United States' entry in World War I were voting in considerable numbers in the several states where they were eligible and were having an increasingly significant impact on the results and on the political scene in general. Voting gave women the power to do more than just indirectly influence men, the power to make their own voices heard.

Chapter 7

Politics and the Suffrage Amendment

For many decades, as we have seen, the woman suffrage movement had had at least some connection with partisan politics. Beginning in the late 1860s, the suffragists had offered to support either of the parties, promising everlasting allegiance to the one that would help them achieve the vote. They at times had participated in campaigns with the hope that the particular party would be grateful and reward them for their contribution. After a while, it had become evident that this strategy was not working: The parties, especially the Republican side, had benefited from women's efforts but had not provided any degree of reciprocation. Nevertheless, some suffrage advocates continued to back their favorite party, believing, as GOP activist J. Ellen Foster did, that this was the best alternative for women and would ultimately lead to their obtaining the franchise. Yet the majority of suffragists, particularly those involved in the reunited National American Woman Suffrage Association (NAWSA) starting in 1890, chose to follow a nonpartisan approach and avoid making any political commitment. They insisted that neutrality was essential in gaining legislative support in the states or building a consensus in Congress for a constitutional amendment. But after 1912 a significant minority would reenter the partisan arena, and, instead of asking for favors, attempted to put pressure on the party in power to hasten passage of a suffrage amendment. As a result, many additional women were thrust into partisan politics via election campaigns, and although the plan as outlined did not fully succeed, it did have a catalytic effect on the process of securing the vote for all women.

This new strategy was made possible by the fact that many more women had recently become eligible voters in the western states. After quite a few years without much progress, the suffrage movement had picked up steam through the work of state and local groups in conjunction with the NAWSA. As we have seen in the previous chapter, by the end of 1912 nine states had admitted women to the full franchise—the original four plus Oregon, Washington, California, Arizona, and Kansas—with Illinois permitting women to vote in subsequent presidential contests. Nationally, this meant that approximately one-fifth of the Senate, one-seventh of the House, and one-sixth of the total electoral vote came from equal suffrage states. It also meant that there were now (along with the 15 million male voters in the United States) about 2 million female voters, not an inconsiderable number.[1]

ALICE PAUL

Given this growing voter base, a small but dedicated group of women's rights advocates led by Alice Paul, who had personally participated in the suffrage movement in England and had been associated with the NAWSA's Congressional Committee, had begun pushing for suffrage in a new manner. Instead of prodding the parties or begging for their support, Paul sought to use the already enfranchised women to influence the election process, holding the party in power responsible for its action or inaction on the suffrage issue. At this time, the Democrats were clearly in the majority—Woodrow Wilson had been elected to the presidency in 1912 and his party controlled both houses of Congress. So Paul attempted to exploit the situation by getting the Democrats either to publicly back the proposed amendment or else suffer the consequences. The Democrats, it should be remembered, had traditionally shown far less interest than the Republicans in female voting rights. With its stronghold in the conservative South, the Democrats had never made even the slightest gesture toward promoting a federal amendment and had always argued that woman suffrage should remain a state matter. Indeed, this position was reaffirmed to Paul and her followers in a meeting with President Wilson soon after he took office in 1913, and by a congressional caucus that asserted its position on the subject early in 1914. As that year's congressional contests grew nearer, Paul, seeing the Democrats' recalcitrant attitude, began putting her scheme into operation. She especially urged western women voters to "withhold their support from the Democratic Party in the national election until that party ceases blocking the suffrage amendment nationally."[2]

This stance immediately created controversy and led to the explusion of Paul's group, the Congressional Union, from the NAWSA, now led by Carrie Chapman Catt. The NAWSA had continued to follow a bipartisan approach so as not to offend the supporters of suffrage in each of the parties and not force women to become partisan if they did not wish to do so. Paul's strategy naturally angered numerous Democrats in Congress, many of whom claimed that by adopting this approach the suffragists had made themselves Republican allies. Paul, however, defended her actions, saying that this was the only way to demonstrate the movement's clout and accomplish its goal. Soon Paul began sending some of her chief associates out west to work with local strategists on the 1914 congressional campaign. Though small in number, the group fought very hard to defeat Democratic candidates in the several states where women voted, and whether from this or other causes, the party had trouble winning. Nevertheless, despite losses in some of the races for Congress, the Democrats increased their majority in the legislatures and in the U.S. Senate from these same western states. Obviously, many western voters, including women, who were partisan Democrats, believed it wrong to punish pro-suffrage Democratic office-seekers simply to make a particular point. But without a doubt, Paul was becoming a thorn in the party's side and beginning to force President Wilson and congressional leaders to take the suffragist reprisal threat seriously.[3] In fact, as a result of the pressure being applied, the Democrats made a few advances toward equal suffrage in the next year and a half.

THE ELECTION OF 1916

Perhaps the two most important advances were President Wilson's announcement by late 1915 that he was personally in favor of woman suffrage and the Democratic national platform's recommendation in mid-1916 of "the extension of the franchise to the women of the country by the States upon the same terms as to men." But if some suffragists saw these steps as consequential, they did not go far enough to satisfy Alice Paul, who wanted more vigorous federal action. Reconstituting her organization as the National Woman's party (NWP), Paul and her followers initiated a much greater effort than two years earlier in trying to defeat the Democrats in the general election of 1916. All over the West, where women now voted in twelve states, the militant suffragists—approximately a few thousand in number—strove to oust the incumbent party. A conference was held in Colorado Springs, Colorado, to formulate strategy for the upcoming race. Party workers were told to explain to women that the Democrats must be defeated because they alone were responsible for the lack of movement on a federal amendment. In every western state, a central agency was set up to coordinate the drive. Press reports were sent out, speaking engagements were arranged, and literature was distributed. Again and again, the slogan "A Vote for the Democratic party is a Vote against Women" was posted on billboards and shouted from the stump.[4]

The National Woman's party was not the only female organization working to defeat President Wilson and the Democrats in 1916. The National Women's Republican Association (NWRA), now headed by Helen Varick Boswell, and an auxiliary group, the Hughes Alliance (named for GOP presidential candidate Charles Evans Hughes), led by former Progressive Frances Kellor, were also trying to oust the incumbent administration. The NWRA aimed its appeal at women of all kinds, "whatever her occupation, condition, or purse." It sought to cover the interests of every woman whether "in industry, in the home, in the suffrage and non-suffrage States," and it adopted the slogan, "Republicanism in the home, in the state, and in the nation." Their goal was to create a coalition that would include suffragists and anti-suffragists who would work together "on the broad ground of the national need for Republican policies and administration." To bring about the election of Hughes and the Republican ticket, the NWRA formed various subgroups such as a 500-member businesswomen's organization. In New York City, a number of committees were created to reach out to women in certain professions such as librarians and secretaries, and one was set up to organize Negro women. The NWRA in 1916 was especially interested in putting together a regional effort in the twelve western states where women could vote and sent an envoy, Miss Doris Stevens, to establish a western headquarters in San Francisco.[5]

To expand their drive for women's votes, the Republicans, in the later stages of the contest, arranged an interesting publicity stunt: the "Hughes Golden Special." This consisted of a trainload of women sent across the country, particularly to the western states, to campaign. This was the first time any female group had ever gone out on a separate partisan electioneering tour. At every stop, they sought to avoid any discussion of the suffrage question. Instead they expressed the need for "women's political cooperation with men for the election of Mr. Hughes in a national crisis," and said they aimed to "unite women in national solidarity behind a national issue." Although tour speakers were sometimes heckled in Democratic strongholds, they generally spoke effectively and received widespread press coverage in each locale. An editorial in the *San Francisco Chronicle* proclaimed that this marked "the beginning of a new era in American politics, one in which women are not merely voters but active molders of public opinion."[6] Nevertheless, for the GOP the trip brought few immediate benefits. The egalitarian women voters in the West did not respond very positively to the Republicans' message or to the fact that it was being delivered by "society ladies" such as Mrs. Payne Whitney and Mrs. Cornelius Vanderbilt, individuals closely associated with Wall Street wealth. Although Democratic "Wilson women" were less organized and not as well financed, they managed to counter the Republican thrust in many places, even invading the Wall Street area of New York City with a speechmaking van.[7]

Another innovative feature of the 1916 presidential contest was a public debate between the parties' leading female campaign organizers, Helen Boswell on the Republican side and Mrs. George Bass from Illinois on the Democratic side. Boswell and Bass faced each other on the stage of Carnegie Hall in New York City before "a large audience of noticeably well-informed women," a few days prior to election day. The debate actually consisted of long statements from the two rivals telling "the good things they knew about their own parties and presidential candidates and the unpleasant things each knew about the opposition." The exciting part came at the close of a question and answer period when the two women spoke on such matters as pure food laws, the war in Europe, and the tariff. On the last point, Boswell claimed that GOP protectionism made the United States into a great industrial nation, while Bass asserted that high tariffs merely protected bloated interests and multimillionaires. Bass also denied that women who supported Wilson during this time of war believed in peace at any price. Speaking with reporters afterward, Bass also criticized the Republican women's campaign train and said that Wilson would carry the female vote in the West. Finally, she condemned the activities of the National Woman's party against Wilson, calling them "idiotic, futile, and militant."[8]

In the end, Wilson and the Democratic party won the election in 1916, with the president capturing ten of the eleven woman suffrage states. This was accomplished despite the fact that Charles Evans Hughes, the GOP candidate, seemed more committed to a federal amendment. The Republicans, perhaps convinced that they were going to win easily in the West, did not campaign there with maximum effort. In addition, the National Woman's party did not prove much help as those involved underestimated their task and could only mobilize a fraction of the region's 2 million women voters. Furthermore, the virtual alliance of Paul's group to the Republican side probably alienated many pro-suffrage women who remained tied to the Democratic party regardless of its foot-dragging on the amendment question. During the campaign too, Carrie Chapman Catt and other leaders of the NAWSA strongly criticized the NWP for its attempt to compel sexual solidarity at the polls and called Alice Paul naive for thinking that she could control the choices of a majority of the women voters. The fact that the NAWSA took a nonpartisan position in the election probably helped the suffrage cause a great deal.[9]

Along with the already mentioned milestones, the year 1916 witnessed the election of the first woman to the United States House of Representatives in the person of Jeannette Rankin of Montana. Rankin, who came from a fairly wealthy family, had graduated from the University of Montana and had also attended the Columbia University School of Social Work. After being employed for a few years as a social worker, she became heavily involved in the woman suffrage movement, and in 1914 she successfully led the campaign to give women the vote in her native state. Two years later, without much organizational support and using a low-key approach—traveling about the state by automobile giving brief speeches and newspaper interviews—Rankin managed to get elected to Congress. Once in Washington, she pushed for passage of the suffrage amendment as well as other legislation aimed at aiding women. A committed pacifist, Rankin was one of several representatives to vote against U.S. entry into the world war, which helped cause her defeat when she sought to win a place in the U.S. Senate in 1918. For the next two decades or so, she dropped out of partisan politics in Montana, but in 1940 she ran again for a House seat and won. A year later, Rankin gained much notoriety as the only member of Congress to oppose the declaration of war against Japan following the attack on Pearl Harbor.[10]

Along with Jeannette Rankin, the first woman to run for the House of Representatives, Anne Martin of Nevada deserves some mention for being the first woman to run for the Senate and for some of her other political activities as well. Martin, the daughter of a prominent Nevada businessman and politician, acquired a graduate degree from Stanford University in history and briefly taught that subject at the University of Nevada. After traveling in Europe and taking an active part in the suffrage movement in England in 1909–1910, she returned to Nevada in 1911, and over the next three years she successfully led the suffrage fight in her home state. Subsequently involved with Alice Paul and the National Woman's party as head of its legislative committee, Martin became frustrated at the slow pace of the struggle for the suffrage amendment and decided to run for a U.S. Senate seat from her home state. She engaged in a vigorous campaign as an independent candidate in both 1918 and 1920, enlisting many prominent suffragists, and received roughly 20 percent of the total vote on each occasion. But the lack of any strong organizational backing and her lukewarm support for America's participation in the world war, as well as her advocacy of federal aid to poor mothers and children, made it difficult for her to do any better at the polls. In later years, Anne Martin was involved in the international peace movement and spoke in favor of an equal rights amendment, but she scrupulously avoided any connection with partisan politics.[11]

WOMEN'S NEW POLITICAL POWER

Women's political activism was not just a far western phenomenon. As various states began granting women their suffrage rights, male politicians started taking steps to recruit women into their party ranks. After New York's statewide referendum had been approved in 1917, New York City district leaders tried to let women know that club houses, where men had always gathered "to smoke and talk politics," were now open to women. The chairman of the New York County Republican Committee went looking for women who could become election district captains, and claimed they would be treated just like the male captains. This meant that on Election Day they were to report for duty at 5:00 A.M. just as the men did. On the Democratic side, district leaders engaged in a lively race with their rivals to win over female voters even to the point of offering at least a few women party jobs. One Democratic organization in midtown Manhattan formed a woman's auxiliary, and its spokesman said that a number of young business and professional types, graduates of Vassar, Barnard, and Hunter, were already doing political work among those of their sex. Although no exact figures are available, estimates show women voting in considerable numbers in the 1918 state primaries and the ensuing general election. On the occasion of the general election, at least 350,000 women voted in New York City and over 1 million cast ballots statewide, comprising 41 percent of the overall total.[12]

New York was not alone in seeing many newly enfranchised women voters immediately go out and exercise their political rights in 1918. In Arkansas, upwards of 40,000 women participated in the state primaries and made their presence felt in the outcome. In Texas, where suffrage opponents had long claimed women did not really want to vote, some 386,000 signed up for that state's primary election. Indeed, in some counties the female registrants outnumbered the males. Even black women registered in those counties in which blacks were not normally excluded. In the small eastern state of Vermont, women were said to have "made good at the polls" in their initial outing, generally voting "about as men do" in what they believed was best for their communities. According to the spokeswoman for the Vermont Equal Suffrage Association:

The attitude in most towns had been very favorable towards the women's voting, the polling places have been improved in many villages, smoking has been abolished, and unpleasant language discontinued. The women who want the ballot, however, take the consequences of the ballot, even though in some instances they have not been agreeable. But an intelligent vote has been cast throughout the state, and it has not been found so difficult after all, nor so unsexing![13]

PASSAGE OF THE NINETEENTH AMENDMENT

Even in states where women did not yet possess the vote the pro-suffrage forces were sometimes able to show their new political clout. Operating in a bipartisan fashion, they were successful in defeating two powerful anti-suffrage senators, John Weeks in Massachusetts and Willard Saulsbury in Delaware. These victories helped push the incoming Congress very close to a pro-suffrage majority and to almost certain submission of the Nineteenth, or Anthony, Amendment to the states. The Republicans now had a majority in the Senate, and since they were more strongly supporting suffrage now—in order to be able to take credit for the impending measure—it eased the way for passage. (Actually, neither party wanted to be seen as responsible for blocking what now seemed inevitable.) By this time, events were moving very rapidly, helped along by the public's growing appreciation for women's year and a half contribution to the war effort on the homefront. President Wilson, in his annual message to Congress in December 1918 a month after the election, called for immediate approval of the suffrage amendment. This was the first time any American president had ever mentioned woman suffrage as part of his legislative program. By May of 1919, Wilson finally obtained the last vote needed to make a two-thirds majority in the Senate so that the amendment could now be formally submitted for ratification by the states. It would then take about fifteen months for the amendment to be ratified by thirty-six of the forty-eight states, Tennessee completing the process in August of 1920.[14]

It was around the time ratification began that Woodrow Wilson, following his months in France negotiating the Versailles Treaty and his subsequent campaign back in this country for the League of Nations, suffered a paralytic stroke that largely incapacitated him. This brings up perhaps the biggest controversy regarding a particular woman's role in the history of American politics: Did President Wilson's second wife, Edith Bolling Wilson, "virtually [take] over the reins of the White House?" Was she, as some have claimed, the assistant president or even acting president during his illness? There is evidence that at this juncture Mrs. Wilson did have influence over which individuals saw her husband and that she read many confidential government reports and communications. Most recent scholars, however, are convinced that she was not running the government. As she herself later wrote: "I studied every paper [but] I myself never made a single decision regarding the disposition of public affairs." Mrs. Wilson had previously not been very political, and she was not disposed to force opinions on the people of this country. If in her position she restricted access to certain persons she did not particularly favor, it was out of concern for her husband's health and well-being and not out of a desire to impose her political will.[15]

THE EFFECTS OF ENFRANCHISEMENT

The enhancement of women's political status from the turn of the century to 1920 can be seen in certain major advances that occurred. There was, for example, a rapid increase in the number of female delegates being chosen to the national party conventions. On the Republican side, the figures rose from three alternate delegates in 1892 to 1 regular delegate in 1900, 4 alternates in 1904, 2 regular delegates in 1908 and 1912, 5 regular delegates and 9 alternates in 1916, and 27 regular and 129 alternate delegates in 1920. In the last instance, 1 woman was appointed to the Committee on Permanent Organization, 4 women were chosen to the Committee on Rules and Order of Business, and 7 spoke to second the nomination of various candidates. The totals for the Democratic party were similar at the outset and yet from 1916 onward wound up somewhat larger. A woman first attended a Democratic convention in 1900. No women obtained selection in 1904, but 2 regular delegates were named in 1908 and 1912, as well as a few alternates. For 1916, the number jumped to 11 delegates and 11 alternates, and for the first time women were appointed to committees, including the credentials committee. By 1920, 93 women served as full convention delegates and 206 received alternate status. Many more Democratic than Republican women were placed on committees that year, and 15 gave seconding speeches. Finally, one female Democrat addressed the entire convention gathering and extolled the party's record in regard to women's interests.[16]

Another area of advancement was obtaining seats on the national committees. Even before the federal suffrage amendment was ratified, the major parties took steps to include women in that regard. As early as 1918, the Republicans placed several women on a national GOP advisory committee, though not on the Republican National Committee itself. The Democrats in 1919 went further in resolving that each state should nominate a woman, who would be an associate member of the Democratic National Committee. The following year, the Democratic convention approved the "fifty-fifty plan of committee representation," whereby the National Committee would consist of a man and a woman from each state, and determined that they should both be elected in the same fashion and be equal in standing. (The Republicans would eventually adopt a similar plan in 1924.) A goodly number of state party committees followed suit, although eight southern and western states refused to go along with the fifty-fifty concept. While some general criticism of the plan arose, especially to the idea that women were to be chosen simply because they were women and that they would be manipulated by the men, the fifty-fifty model did give a number of women entrance into high-level politics. Moreover, this system helped accustom many male politicians to working with members of the opposite sex. On the other hand, this system, by forcing women into the party picture regardless of whether or not they were welcome, may have antagonized men toward women in politics even more than was already the case.[17]

THE ELECTION OF 1920

When the federal amendment was approved in the summer of 1920, almost all adult women throughout the country became eligible for the upcoming presidential vote. In response, both major parties initiated massive efforts to capture the new voter, far beyond what they had done in the few western states years earlier. Huge amounts of campaign literature were for the first time aimed at women. The parties began making promises to appoint women to high government posts. They also started nominating women as candidates for elective office, although as would become a trend over time, it was usually for positions they had little chance of winning. In addition, women were employed in more aspects of campaigning than before, and more female speakers than ever were out on the hustings, especially addressing women's groups. Among the speakers was Edith Roosevelt, wife of the recently deceased ex-president, and Florence Harding, wife of the Republican presidential nominee. Mrs. Harding, in fact, gave a good account of herself wherever she spoke. On the other hand, Mrs. James Cox, the wife of the Democratic candidate did not campaign. "I don't know politics. I admit it," she said. She was not alone. Getting the newly enfranchised voter to overcome past restraints and participate was not always easy. Many women claimed they did not feel qualified to vote. However, as one Republican organizer put it: "We must make them [feel] qualified."[18]

During the election, each party sought to show that it welcomed women and would serve women better than its opponent. Each party's spokesmen claimed that their side had done the most to bring women the vote. The Democrats insisted that the Wilson administration had made the amendment's approval possible, while the Republicans argued that the GOP provided the bulk of support in Congress and in the ratifying states. Each party also declared that it was the stronger of the two in supporting legislation favorable to women and protective of the home. The Democrats pointed to the party platform, which included twelve of the fifteen resolutions proposed by the newly formed nonpartisan League of Women Voters. Meanwhile, Republican presidential nominee Warren Harding went beyond the limited platform proposal of his party by calling for equal pay for equal work, an eight-hour day, an end to child labor, the enforcement of prohibition, maternity and infancy protection, and an extension of the Children's Bureau. As the campaign progressed, Harding and the Republicans clearly outdistanced the Democrats in the scope of their appeal, even holding a special Woman's Day where the candidate hosted numerous women's groups at his home. Harding was, of course, elected in a landslide over the Democratic standard-bearer James Cox.[19]

Harding's landslide victory, coming immediately after the suffrage amendment, for a long time encouraged the view that women voters were responsible for his success. Thus, when Harding's administration was rocked with scandal, this too was used against women. But were women really a significant factor in Harding's victory? Did far greater numbers of women than men vote for Harding, a person of distinguished appearance perceived as the "moral" candidate? Many contemporaries believed they did elect him. As evidence, they cited the voting results in Illinois, the only state with a separate male/female count, where proportionately more women did vote Republican. However, a recent analysis of the 1920 election tally by Sara Alpern and Dale Baum indicates a more varied pattern nationally. Although the women's vote in the mid-Atlantic states (along with Illinois) helped augment Harding's majorities, Alpern and Baum show that in New England and in the Midwest (outside of Illinois), "women who voted were not more demonstrably in the Republican column than were their [male] counterparts at the polls." Yet this study also makes clear that women did not simply go along with their father's, brother's, or husband's advice and that their vote was not an exact mirror of men's. At the same time, the returns in most states give no evidence of a sharply delineated gender vote on the presidential level, in contrast to some predictions to the contrary.[20]

Below the presidential level, voting by newly enfranchised women did not bring about great changes either. In a few widely publicized contests against longtime suffrage foes, the attempts to oust them failed. In heavily Republican Connecticut, where the state's Woman Suffrage Association called on the voters to "Place Principle above Party" and defeat conservative Senator Frank Brandegee, the plea was rejected and Brandegee won. In New York, despite a strong campaign against Republican Senator James Wadsworth, whose wife had headed the National Association against Woman Suffrage, Wadsworth won. Women voters also proved unable to protect a number of pro-suffrage friends. Democratic Governor A. H. Roberts of Tennessee, who had called the special session of the legislature that had made possible the final ratification of the Nineteenth Amendment, lost his post. It was in that state, ironically, that the opposing Republicans did more to encourage women to vote their ticket, which made the difference. Of course, the pro-suffrage forces did score some victories. One of them was the retention of Harry Burn, the twenty-four-year-old Tennessee legislator, who that summer had changed his vote (to please his mother, it was said) in order to bring about ratification of the suffrage amendment. The party organization in his district had sought to punish him and refused him backing, but thanks to the aid provided by women of both sides in the area, Burn was reelected.[21]

THE EARLY POST-SUFFRAGE PERIOD

From the feminist point of view, the election of 1920, with its rather mixed results, did not bring too much satisfaction, foreshadowing the situation of women in politics over the next half-century. Especially in the decade immediately following the suffrage amendment, achievements did not coincide with expectations. The female vote remained somewhat lower than the male vote, women's success at obtaining public office was not at all common, and advancement in the party structure proceeded at a very slow pace. Several commentators at the time remarked on what appeared to be "politics as usual" throughout the country, with no reform in sight. To them nothing had changed except "the number of docile ballot-droppers." One woman organizer wrote that "in the heart of many a good suffragist there is a little sickening sense of disappointment; in the mind of the conscienceless boss, there is a very genuine sense of relief."[22] The limited gains made by women in the years after 1920 may well have contributed to the later impression of an almost nonexistent female presence in the partisan realm before 1920. Yet as the foregoing pages make clear, this notion can be dismissed: women did indeed play a part in partisan politics, and an increasingly significant one in many respects.

Why, however, given women's political performance prior to 1920, did it not lead to their having a much greater impact immediately after that date? To answer this question, several factors must be considered.[23] First, as certain contemporaries themselves understood, once the suffrage amendment was approved, an important symbol of women's political struggle no longer existed. It would prove difficult to maintain the spirit developed in the previous generation without a similar goal. Then, too, many women took future progress for granted and felt little need to continue serving in an active political role. Female voters, they assumed, would naturally vote for "good government" candidates so that not much extra work would be necessary. Furthermore, as women now sought places of power on a broad basis, men displayed a strong reluctance to make concessions of any substance. It was one thing to employ members of the opposite sex as party auxiliaries and speakers, but it was quite another to give the newcomers positions of real authority. As one longtime activist put it in 1923: "Men don't share anything with them. The politicians just hand them all-day suckers. They give them busy work."[24] In addition, women entering electoral politics at this juncture were doing so when the importance of accomplishing change through the ballot box had already passed its peak. Mass mobilization during campaigns was on the decline, political parties were starting to lose some of their influence, and government was beginning to respond more to individual pressure groups regarding legislation.[25] Also, some of the new women, having made their initial contact with partisan activities, found that they wanted nothing more to do with male-led organizations that sometimes used what seemed to them unsavory tactics. One Indiana businesswoman interviewed by Robert and Helen Lynd for their "Middletown" study, declared that her experience "thoroughly disgusted me with politics," leaving no desire to pursue it again.[26] Indeed, numerous women of this type apparently reverted to the nineteenth-century model of working through voluntary associations to achieve their goals.

Of course, many female activists never formed attachments to the partisan realm in the first place. Immediately after the suffrage amendment was passed, quite a few joined the League of Women Voters (LWV), which grew out of the National American Woman Suffrage Association (NAWSA). Some of its leaders, like former NAWSA president Carrie Chapman Catt, hoped to use women's new political power in conjunction with the regular parties, but the majority believed that women's special voice would be lost in such a move. It was eventually decided that the League should remain nonpartisan, support general programs of reform, and promote political education.[27] The National Woman's party also distanced itself from partisan politics, feeling that any chance to pursue issues vital to women would inevitably be sacrificed. By becoming part of the existing male-dominated system, Anne Martin exclaimed, women would wind up "exactly where men political leaders wanted them, bound, gagged, divided, and delivered to the Republican and Democratic parties."[28] Unlike the LWV, Alice Paul and the Woman's party wished to focus exclusively on women's rights measures, and so in 1923 they first proposed the idea of an equal rights amendment. This proposal would cause serious divisions among women in the political sphere for almost half a century and would soon push the NWP even further from the mainstream.[29] In addition, from the standpoint of the women who were already involved in partisan politics, both the NWP and the LWV took away potentially important figures and thereby slowed women's overall political progress.

Yet the picture of post-suffrage women in the partisan realm was not as bleak as some contemporaries and later historians have painted it. Women did, in fact, make certain tangible gains. If we look at actual political results in the 1920s, we find, for example, that the gap between men's and women's voting percentages narrowed considerably by the end of the decade. Whereas a 25 percent difference probably existed at the outset, it was down to 20 and even 10 percent in some states by 1930.[30] In terms of officeholding, while women in public positions were still the exception, as an LWV study that year demonstrated, one could already observe "an impressive array of exceptions." Besides thousands of minor officials, two women state governors—Nellie Tayloe Ross in Wyoming and Miriam "Ma" Ferguson in Texas—and 149 state legislators had been elected. There had also been two state auditors, two state treasurers, and six secretaries of state. On the municipal level, people had elected a dozen women mayors—including one (Bertha Landes) in the sizable city of Seattle—as well as a city alderman in Cleveland, several judges, and numerous city clerks.[31]

Political gains for women could be seen within the partisan realm itself as well. As Sarah Butler, daughter of the president of Columbia University and a member of the New York State Republican Committee, noted in an essay written to assess women's political achievements by 1930, progress needed to be measured by the large number of women who had made a recognized place for themselves in party ranks. As she pointed out, by this time "even the most hardened party leaders have begun to realize that in their plans of campaign strategy they must take the woman voter into account."[32] The women's division in each party was upgraded and was making a more diligent effort to mobilize women voters. Indeed, two women had been given major positions by their respective party organizations in the 1928 presidential race. The Democrats put former social worker and legislative adviser Belle Moscowitz in charge of publicity for Al Smith, and the Republicans placed lawyer and Assistant Attorney General Mabel Willebrandt in a high-level post to promote the election of Herbert Hoover.[33] Thus, women were building substantially on their pre–1920 achievements in the post–1920 decade, setting the stage for further gains in the years to come.

The next few decades, from the 1930s through the 1950s, saw some advances for women in partisan politics. The gap in voter participation continued to diminish to a point where it was almost negligible. Within the political parties, women gained greater representation on platform committees and other important bodies. To broaden their base of female support, both parties' national organizations would expand their women's divisions in the 1930s. Under the leadership of Molly W. Dewson on the Democratic side, many new local clubs and statewide groups were formed. There were also many more women placed in high government posts, most notably Frances Perkins, a former social worker whose appointment as Secretary of Labor by Franklin Roosevelt made her the first woman cabinet member. For the first time, women were named to federal judgeships and ambassadorial positions. Women increased their numbers in elected offices as well, especially on the municipal level. Yet in many respects changes were minimal. Men still held almost all of the power in government and only a handful of women ever sat in either the House or Senate. No feminist vision or movement spurred any significant alteration in attitude, and it would not be until the women's liberation movement in the 1960s, over four decades after women obtained the vote, that there would be any stirrings in that direction.[34]

Notes

INTRODUCTION

1. Eleanor Roosevelt and Lorena Hickok, *Ladies of Courage* (New York, 1954).

2. Mary Beth Norton, *Liberty's Daughters: The Revolutionary Experience of American Women, 1750–1800* (Boston, 1980); Linda K. Kerber, *Women of the Republic: Intellect and Ideology in Revolutionary America* (Chapel Hill, N.C., 1980); Mary P. Ryan, *Women in Public: Between Banners and Ballots, 1825–1880* (Baltimore, 1990); Lori D. Ginzberg, *Women and the Work of Benevolence: Morality, Politics, and Class in the Nineteenth-Century United States* (New Haven, Conn., 1990); Barbara L. Epstein, *The Politics of Domesticity: Women, Evangelism, and Temperance in Nineteenth-Century America* (Middletown, Conn., 1981); Ruth Bordin, *Women and Temperance: The Quest for Power and Liberty, 1873–1900* (Philadelphia, 1981); Mari Jo Buhle, *Women and American Socialism, 1870–1920* (Urbana, Ill., 1981).

3. Paula Baker, "The Domestication of Politics: Women and American Political Society, 1780–1920," *American Historical Review* 89 (June 1984): 620–47.

4. Michael McGerr, "Political Style and Women's Power, 1830–1930," *Journal of American History* 77 (December 1990): 864–95.

5. Suzanne Lebsock, "Women and American Politics, 1880–1920," in Louise A. Tilly and Patricia Gurin, eds., *Women, Politics, and Change* (New York, 1990), pp. 35–62.

6. I wish to thank Paula Baker for providing me with this point. Letter to author, December 1992.

7. See, for example, the experience in one state in Michael L. Goldberg, "Non-Partisan and All-Partisan: Rethinking Woman Suffrage and Party Politics in Gilded Age Kansas," *Western Historical Quarterly* 25 (Spring 1994): 21–44.

8. Quoted in Richard Stiller, *Queen of the Populists: The Story of Mary Lease* (New York, 1970), p. 136.

CHAPTER 1

1. For women's role, see Edmund S. Morgan, *The Puritan Family* (New York, 1966), p. 42. See also Benjamin Wadsworth, *The Well-Ordered Family* (Boston, 1712), p. 35, from which the quotation comes.

2. John Cotton, *Discourse about Civil Government* (Cambridge, Mass., 1663), p. 5.

3. *The Polite Lady*, 3d ed. (London, 1775), quoted in Julia Cherry Spruill, *Women's Life and Work in the Southern Colonies* (Chapel Hill, N.C., 1938), p. 244.

4. John Adams to John Sullivan, May 26, 1776, in Charles F. Adams, ed., *The Works of John Adams*, 10 vols. (Boston, 1850–56), 9: 376.

5. Robert J. Dinkin, *Voting in Provincial America: A Study of Elections in the Thirteen British Colonies, 1689–1776* (Westport, Conn., 1977), p. 30; *New York Gazette*, June 6, 1737.

6. Albert E. McKinley, *The Suffrage Franchise in the Thirteen British Colonies in America* (Philadelphia, 1905), pp. 53–54, 192–93.

7. Quoted in Dinkin, *Voting in Provincial America*, p. 101.

8. Linda K. Kerber, *Women of the Republic: Intellect and Ideology in Revolutionary America* (Chapel Hill, N.C., 1980), pp. 8–9.

9. Ibid., pp. 36–37.

10. Laurel Thatcher Ulrich, " 'Daughters of Liberty': Religious Women in Revolutionary New England," in Ronald Hoffman and Peter J. Albert, eds., *Women in the Age of the American Revolution* (Charlottesville, Va., 1989), pp. 211–43; Mary Beth Norton, *Liberty's Daughters: The Revolutionary Experience of American Women, 1750–1800* (Boston, 1980), pp. 166–69.

11. *Providence Gazette*, March 12, 1766, quoted in Ulrich, "Daughters of Liberty," p. 215.

12. Quoted in Norton, *Liberty's Daughters*, p. 167.

13. Quoted in Kerber, *Women of the Republic*, p. 41.

14. Ibid., pp. 85–89.

15. Ibid., pp. 99–110; Norton, *Liberty's Daughters*, pp. 178–87.

16. Robert J. Dinkin, *Voting in Revolutionary America: A Study of Elections in the Original Thirteen States, 1776–1789* (Westport, Conn., 1982), p. 42.

17. [Theophilus Parsons], *Results of the Convention of Delegates Holden at Ipswich in the County of Essex* (Newburyport, Mass., 1778), p. 29.

18. Quoted in Mary S. Benson, *Women in Eighteenth-Century America* (New York, 1935), p. 246.

19. James C. Ballagh, ed., *The Letters of Richard Henry Lee*, 2 vols. (New York, 1914), 1: 392–94.

20. Caroline Gilman, ed., *Letters of Eliza Wilkinson* (New York, 1839; reprint, 1969), p. 17. For a general look at women's political opinions during the American Revolution, see Kerber, *Women of the Republic*, pp. 73–85.

21. Quoted in Kerber, *Women of the Republic*, pp. 78, 79.

22. Quoted in Joan Hoff-Wilson, "The Illusion of Change: Women and the American Revolution," in Alfred F. Young, ed., *The American Revolution: Explorations in the History of American Radicalism* (DeKalb, Ill., 1976), p. 391. For the life and writings of Mercy Otis Warren, see Katharine Anthony, *First Lady of the Revolution* (Garden City, N.Y., 1958).

23. Kerber, *Women of the Republic*, pp. 82–84. The quotation is on p. 83.

24. Abigail Adams to John Adams, March 31, 1776, in Lyman H. Butterfield et al., eds., *Adams Family Correspondence*, 6 vols. (Cambridge, Mass., 1963–1993), 1: 370.

25. Abigail Adams to John Adams, July 5, 1780, in ibid., 3: 372.

26. Ibid. For a discussion of her political views, see Edith B. Gelles, *Portia: The World of Abigail Adams* (Bloomington, Ind., 1992), pp. 125–29, and Linda G. De Pauw, "The American Revolution and the Rights of Women: The Feminist Theory of Abigail Adams," in Larry R. Gerlach, ed., *Legacies of the American Revolution* (Logan, Utah, 1978), pp. 199–219.

27. Abigail Adams to Mary Cranch, in Stewart Mitchell, ed., *New Letters of Abigail Adams, 1788–1801* (Boston, 1947), p. 112.

28. Quoted in Janet Whitney, *Abigail Adams* (Boston, 1947), p. 290.

29. Hoff-Wilson, "Illusion of Change," p. 419.

30. On Republican motherhood, see Kerber, *Women of the Republic*, chap. 9.

31. *Pennsylvania Gazette*, June 6, 1787, quoted in Benson, *Women in Eighteenth-Century America*, p. 168.

32. *Observations on the New Constitution by a Columbian Patriot* (Boston, 1788). See also Larry M. Lane and Judith J. Lane, "The Columbian Patriot: Mercy Otis Warren and the Constitution," *Women & Politics* 10 (April 1990): 17–29.

33. Winslow C. Watson, ed., *Men and Times of the Revolution, or Memoirs of Elkanah Watson* (New York, 1856), p. 251.

CHAPTER 2

1. Ferdinand M. Bayard, *Travels of a Frenchman in Maryland and Virginia* (Ann Arbor, Mich., 1950), p. 66.

2. Mary Philbrook, "Woman Suffrage in New Jersey," New Jersey Historical Society *Proceedings* 57 (1939): 87–98; Irwin N. Gertzog, "Female Suffrage in New Jersey, 1790–1807," *Women & Politics* 10 (April 1990): 47–58; Judith A. Klinghoffer and Lois Elkis, " 'The Petticoat Electors': Women's Suffrage in New Jersey, 1776–1807," *Journal of the Early Republic* 12 (Summer 1992): 159–93.

3. Mary E. Dewey, ed., *Life and Letters of Catharine Sedgwick* (New York, 1872), p. 34.

4. Mary Beth Norton, *Liberty's Daughters: The Revolutionary Experience of American Women, 1750–1800* (Boston, 1980), p. 189.

5. "Constantia," no. 87, "The Acrimony of Party Spirit Lamented," *Massachusetts Magazine*, December 1, 1796. On the life of Judith Sargent Murray, see Janet W. James, *Changing Ideas about Women in the United States, 1776–1825* (New York, 1981), pp. 104–12.

6. Quoted in De Alva S. Alexander, *A Political History of the State of New York* (New York, 1906), 1: 215. See also David H. Fischer, *The Revolution of American Conservatism: The Federalist Party in the Era of Jeffersonian Democracy* (New York, 1965), p. 15.

7. Quoted in Fischer, *Revolution*, pp. 124, 184.

8. Quoted in Noble E. Cunningham, "Presidential Leadership, Political Parties, and the Congressional Caucus, 1800–1824," in Patricia Bonomi et al., eds., *The American Constitutional System under Strong and Weak Parties* (New York, 1981), p. 7.

9. Dolley Madison to James Madison, November 1, 1805, in *Memoirs and Letters of Dolley Madison* (Boston, 1886), pp. 60–61.

10. On Louisa Adams, see Betty Boyd Caroli, *First Ladies* (New York, 1987), pp. 19–24. The quotations are on pp. 23, 24.

11. Margaret Bayard Smith, *The First Forty Years of Washington Society*, ed. by Gaillard Hunt (New York, 1906; reprint 1965).

12. Ibid., p. 148. See also William C. Bruce, *John Randolph of Roanoke, 1773–1833: A Biography*, 2 vols. (New York, 1922), 2: 417.

13. Smith, *First Forty Years*, pp. 145, 184–85, 212, 310.

14. Leon Phillips, *That Eaton Woman* (New York, 1974), pp. 104, 133–34.

15. Bessie R. James, *Anne Royall's U.S.A.* (New Brunswick, N.J., 1972), esp. pp. 197, 206, 259, 312–14, 322, 327–28, 344–45. The quotation is on p. 314.

16. Celia Morris Eckhardt, *Fanny Wright: Rebel in America* (Cambridge, Mass., 1984), esp. pp. 216–17, 258.

17. Alexis de Tocqueville, *Democracy in America*, 2 vols. ed. by Phillips Bradley (New York, 1945), 1: 250.

18. Quoted in Keith Melder, *Beginnings of Sisterhood: The American Woman's Rights Movement, 1800–1850* (New York, 1977), p. 35.

19. *New York Herald*, October 17, November 3, 1838.

20. Susan McWhorter to James Polk, June 22, 1838, in Herbert Weaver, ed., *Correspondence of James K. Polk*, 7 vols. (Nashville, Tenn., 1969–1989), 4: 487.

21. Caroli, *First Ladies*, pp. 59–62.

22. Catherine Clinton, *The Plantation Mistress: Woman's World in the Old South* (New York, 1983), pp. 181–82. See also Eugene D. Genovese, "Toward a Kinder and Gentler America: The Southern Lady in the Greening of the Politics of the Old South," in Carol Bleser, ed., *In Joy and in Sorrow: Women, Family, and Marriage in the Victorian South* (New York, 1991), pp. 125–34.

23. John C. Calhoun to Anna Maria Calhoun, March 10, 1832, in Robert L. Meriwether et al., eds., *The Papers of John C. Calhoun*, 21 vols. (Columbia, S.C., 1959–), 11: 562.

24. J. S. Buckingham, *The Slave States of America*, 2 vols. (London, 1842), 2: 182–83.

25. Mary P. Ryan, *Women in Public: Between Banners and Ballots, 1825–1880* (Baltimore, 1990), chap. 3; Lori D. Ginzberg, *Women and the Work of Benevolence: Morality, Politics, and Class in the Nineteenth-Century United States* (New Haven, Conn., 1990), chaps. 1–3.

26. Gilbert H. Barnes, *The Anti-Slavery Crusade, 1830–1844* (Washington, D.C., 1933), pp. 130–45; Gerda Lerner, *The Grimke Sisters from South Carolina* (Boston, 1967), pp. 270–75.

27. For the life and work of Lydia Maria Child, see Milton Meltzer, *Tongue of Flame: The Life of Lydia Maria Child* (New York, 1965).

28. For the life and work of Lucretia Mott, see Margaret H. Bacon, *Valiant Friend: The Life of Lucretia Mott* (New York, 1980).

29. Lerner, *Grimke Sisters*, pp. 165–69.

30. Quoted in ibid., p. 7.

31. Ginzberg, *Women and the Work of Benevolence*, p. 85.

32. *New England Spectator*, July 12, 1837, reprinted in Larry Ceplair, ed., *The Public Years of Sarah and Angelina Grimke* (New York, 1989), p. 211.

33. Quoted in Lerner, *Grimke Sisters*, p. 193.

34. Speech of John Quincy Adams (1838), quoted in Linda K. Kerber, *Women of the Republic: Intellect and Ideology in Revolutionary America* (Chapel Hill, N.C., 1980), p. 112.

35. Quoted in Barnes, *Anti-Slavery Impulse*, p. 143.

36. Lerner, *Grimke Sisters*, p. 274. Lori Ginzberg, *Women and the Work of Benevolence*, pp. 69–70, states that women at this time were beginning to live "with the contradictions of exerting their influence in decidedly political ways toward clearly political ends."

37. Quoted in Carl Degler, *At Odds: Women and the Family in America from the Revolution to the Present* (New York, 1980), p. 336.

38. Quoted in Robert G. Gunderson, *The Log-Cabin Campaign* (Lexington, Ky., 1957), pp. 137, 138.

39. *North Carolina Standard*, October 28, 1840, quoted in Guion G. Johnson, *Ante-Bellum North Carolina: A Social History* (Chapel Hill, N.C., 1937), p. 249.

40. D. C. Bloomer, *Life and Writings of Amelia Bloomer* (Boston, 1895; reprint New York, 1975), pp. 17–18.

41. Gunderson, *Log-Cabin Campaign*, p. 136.

42. Quoted in ibid., pp. 137–38.

43. *Washington Globe*, February 1, 1839, quoted in Elbert B. Smith, *Francis Preston Blair* (New York, 1980), p. 129.

44. *North Carolina Standard*, October 28, 1840, quoted in Johnson, *Ante-Bellum North Carolina*, p. 249.

45. Jayne Crumpler DeFiore, "COME, and Bring the Ladies: Tennessee Women and the Politics of Opportunity during the Presidential Campaigns of 1840 and 1844," *Tennessee Historical Quarterly* 51 (Winter 1992): 197–212. The quotation is on p. 201.

46. Ryan, *Women in Public*, pp. 135–37.

47. Jean G. Hales, " 'Co-Laborers in the Cause': Women in the Ante-Bellum Nativist Movement," *Civil War History* 25 (June 1979): 119–38.

48. Ibid., esp. pp. 132–34.

49. Marvin E. Gettleman, *The Dorr Rebellion: A Study in American Radicalism, 1843–1849* (New York, 1973), esp. p. 168n.

50. Thomas Dublin, *Women at Work* (New York, 1978), pp. 109–16. The quotation is on p. 115.

51. Ibid., p. 200.

52. On the decline of women's participation, see DeFiore, "COME, and Bring the Ladies," pp. 208–10. On the election of 1848, see Joseph Raybeck, *Free Soil: The Election of 1848* (Lexington, Ky., 1971). On the importance of the Seneca Falls Convention and its radical request for woman suffrage, see Ellen C. DuBois, *Feminism and Suffrage: The Emergence of an Independent Women's Movement in America, 1848–1869* (Ithaca, N.Y., 1978).

CHAPTER 3

1. For a discussion of the general political developments in this period, see David M. Potter, *The Impending Crisis, 1848–1861* (New York, 1976); Michael F. Holt, *The Political Crisis of the 1850s* (New York, 1978); and William E. Gienapp, *The Origins of the Republican Party, 1852–1856* (New York, 1987).

2. Some of these subjects are dealt with at length in Lori D. Ginzberg, *Women and the Work of Benevolence: Morality, Politics, and Class in the Nineteenth-Century United States* (New Haven, Conn., 1990).

3. Ibid., chap. 4, and Lori D. Ginzberg, "'Moral Suasion Is Moral Balderdash': Women, Politics, and Social Activism in the 1850s," *Journal of American History* 73 (December 1986): 602.

4. Ginzberg, "Moral Suasion," p. 604.

5. Quoted in ibid., pp. 604–5.

6. Quoted in Charles M. Snyder, *The Lady and the President* (Lexington, Ky., 1975), p. 14.

7. Mary P. Ryan, *Women in Public: Between Banners and Ballots, 1825–1880* (Baltimore, 1990), p. 106.

8. "Female Politicians," *Democratic Review* (April 1852): 356.

9. Ibid., p. 356.

10. Ibid., pp. 357–58.

11. Henry Ward Beecher, Speech at the Cooper Union, *New York Times*, February 3, 1860.

12. Ibid. For two additional examples of contemporary statements by men in defense of women in partisan politics, see Theodore Parker, "A Sermon on the Public Function of Woman" (1853), and Ralph Waldo Emerson, "Woman" (1855), reprinted in Michael S. Kimmel and Thomas E. Mosmiller, eds., *Against the Tide: Pro-Feminist Men in the United States, 1776–1990—A Documentary History* (Boston, 1992), pp. 214–20.

13. Quoted in Catherine C. Phillips, *Cornelius Cole, California Pioneer and United States Senator* (San Francisco, 1929), p. 90.

14. Quoted in William E. Gienapp, "Politics Seem to Enter into Everything," in Stephen E. Maizlish and John J. Kushma, eds., *Essays on American Antebellum Politics, 1840–1860* (College Station, Tex., 1982), p. 17.

15. Julia Ward Howe, *Reminiscences 1818–1899* (Boston, 1899), pp. 218–19.

16. Quoted in Gienapp, "Politics Seem to Enter," p. 17.

17. Forrest Wilson, *Crusader in Crinoline: The Life of Harriet Beecher Stowe* (Philadelphia, 1941), chap. 6.

18. "Appeal to the Women of the Free States," reprinted in Jeanne Boydston et al., *The Limits of Sisterhood: The Beecher Sisters on Women's Rights and Women's Sphere* (Chapel Hill, N.C., 1988), pp. 180–83.

19. Gordon Kleeberg, *Formation of the Republican Party* (New York, 1911), p. 15.

20. *John Sherman's Recollections of Forty Years in the House, Senate and Cabinet*, 2 vols. (Chicago, 1895), 1: 104.

21. Elizabeth Cady Stanton to Susan B. Anthony, November 4, 1855, in *Elizabeth Cady Stanton, As Revealed in Her Letters, Diary, and Reminiscences*, 2 vols., ed. by Theodore Stanton and Harriot Stanton Blatch (New York, 1922), 2: 62.

22. Pamela Herr, *Jessie Benton Frémont* (New York, 1987), pp. 260–61; *New York Times*, July 21, 1856; George Julian, *Political Recollections, 1840 to 1872* (Chicago, 1884), p. 154.

23. Milton Meltzer and Patricia G. Holland, eds., *Lydia Maria Child: Selected Letters, 1817–1880* (Amherst, Mass., 1982), pp. 210, 240, 283–87, 289, 291, 295.

24. "Clarina Nichols," in Edward T. James, Janet W. James, and Paul Boyer, eds., *Notable American Women, 1607–1950*, 3 vols. (Cambridge, Mass., 1971), 2: 625–27 (hereafter cited as *NAW*).

25. *Civil War Nurse: The Diary and Letters of Hannah Ropes* ed. by John R. Brumgardt (Knoxville, Tenn., 1962), pp. 12–22.

26. Allan Nevins, *Frémont: The West's Greatest Adventurer*, 2 vols. (New York, 1928), 2: 496–97. For her role in her husband's campaign, see Herr, *Jessie Benton Frémont*, chap. 18.

27. *New York Times*, October 10, 17, 1856. The quotation appears in Herr, *Jessie Benton Frémont*, p. 263.

28. M. B. Schnapper, *Grand Old Party: The First Hundred Years of the Republican Party* (Washington, D.C., 1955), p. 38. See also Stefan Lorant, *Lincoln: A Picture History of His Life* (New York, 1969). On women attending the debates, see John Mack Faragher, *Sugar Creek: Life on the Illinois Prairie* (New Haven, Conn., 1986), p. 214.

29. On Mary Todd Lincoln, see Ruth P. Randall, *Mary Lincoln: Biography of a Marriage* (Boston, 1953), esp. pp. 28–29, and Jean H. Baker, *Mary Todd Lincoln: A Biography* (New York, 1987). The quotation is taken from Baker's essay, "Mary Todd Lincoln," in G. J. Barker-Benfield and Catherine Clinton, eds., *Portraits of American Women* (New York, 1991), p. 248. On Adele Cutts Douglas, see Robert W. Johannsen, *Stephen A. Douglas* (New York, 1973), pp. 542, 620, 655, 777, 778.

30. For the life of Anna Carroll, see Janet L. Coryell, *Neither Heroine nor Fool: Anna Ella Carroll of Maryland* (Kent, Ohio, 1990), esp. chaps. 1–4, and Charles M. Snyder, "Anna Ella Carroll, Political Strategist and Gadfly of President Fillmore," *Maryland Historical Magazine* 68 (Spring 1973): 36–63. Jean G. Hales, "'Co-Laborers in the Cause': Women in the Antebellum Nativist Movement," *Civil War History* 25 (June 1979): 137, is the source for the quotations from *The Great American Battle*.

31. Julius Silberger, *Mary Baker Eddy* (Boston, 1980), esp. pp. 20, 35, 49, 57, 207n.

32. For Louisa McCord, see the biographical sketch in Margaret F. Thorp, *Female Persuasion: Six Strong-Minded Women* (New Haven, Conn., 1949), pp. 179–214, esp. pp. 204–8.

33. Julia Gardiner Tyler, "Reply to the Duchess of Sutherland and Other Ladies of England," reprinted in Mary Beard, *America Through Women's Eyes* (New York, 1933), pp. 136–41. The quotation can be found on p. 138.

34. The entire exchange can be read in *Letters of Lydia Maria Child* (Boston, 1883; reprint New York, 1969), pp. 120–37.

35. On Jane Swisshelm, see Arthur J. Larson, ed., *Crusader and Feminist: Letters of Jane Grey Swisshelm, 1858–1865* (St. Paul, Minn., 1934; reprint Westport, Conn., 1976), introduction, esp. pp. 22–23.

36. *Independent*, November 15, 1860, quoted in Wendy Hamand Venet, *Neither Ballots nor Bullets: Women Abolitionists and the Civil War* (Charlottesville, Va., 1991), p. 22.

37. Mary A. Livermore, *My Story of the War* (Hartford, Conn., 1890), pp. 550–51; *New York Times*, September 13, 1860; *Chicago Tribune*, September 3, 7, October 13, 17, 1860. "Wide Awakes" were originally all-male marching companies formed to promote the election of Republicans. Members wore colorful outfits including oilcloth capes to protect them from the fuel dripping out of their torches. The term Wide Awake comes from the idea that the group was highly aware of the crisis caused by the spread of slavery.

38. Johannsen, *Douglas*, p. 777.

39. Willard L. King, *Lincoln's Manager, David Davis* (Cambridge, Mass., 1960), p. 160.

40. *The Personal Memoirs of Julia Dent Grant*, ed. by John Y. Simon (New York, 1975), p. 86.

41. George C. Rable, *Civil Wars: Women and the Crisis of Southern Nationalism* (Urbana, Ill., 1989), p. 43; Mary Elizabeth Massey, *Bonnet Brigades* (New York, 1966), pp. 25–26.

42. Mrs. Roger A. [Adele] Pryor, *Reminiscences of Peace and War* (New York, 1904), pp. 98–99.

43. Francis B. Simkins and James W. Patton, *The Women of the Confederacy* (Richmond, Va., 1936), pp. 8–11.

44. Adele Petrigru Allston to Mrs. Joseph Hunter, May 15, 1861, in J. H. Easterby, ed., *The South Carolina Rice Plantation, As Revealed in the Papers of Robert F. W. Allston* (Chicago, 1945), pp. 175; Simkins and Patton, *Women of the Confederacy*, pp. 10–11.

45. Samuel Proctor, ed., "The Call to Arms: Secession from a Feminine Point of View," *Florida Historical Quarterly* 35 (January 1957): 266–70.

46. H. E. Sterkx, *Partners in the Rebellion: Alabama Women in the Civil War* (Rutherford, N.J., 1970), pp. 23–25.

47. Drew Gilpin Faust, "Altars of Sacrifice: Confederate Women and the Narratives of War," *Journal of American History* 76 (March 1990): 1206.

48. Quoted in Sterkx, *Partners in the Rebellion*, pp. 39–40.

49. Rable, *Civil Wars*, p. 144.

50. Ibid., p. 144–51.

51. Quoted in Elizabeth Cady Stanton et al., eds., *History of Woman Suffrage*, 6 vols. (Rochester and New York, 1881–1922), 2: 882.

52. Quoted in ibid., p. 875.

53. Venet, *Neither Ballots nor Bullets*, p. 102.

54. Kathleen L. Endres, "The Women's Press in the Civil War," *Civil War History* 30 (March 1984): 31–53.

55. On women's relief work during the war, see Ginzberg, *Women and the Work of Benevolence*, chap. 5, and George M. Frederickson, *The Inner Civil War: Northern Intellectuals and the Crisis of the Union* (New York, 1965), chap. 7.

56. Venet, *Neither Ballots nor Bullets*, chap. 5.

57. Ibid., chap. 6. The quotations are found on pp. 132, 133.

58. For Anna Dickinson, see Giraud Chester, *Embattled Maiden: The Life of Anna Dickinson* (New York, 1951), esp. chap. 4; Massey, *Bonnet Brigades*, chap. 8; Venet, *Neither Ballots nor Bullets*, pp. 37–56, 124–29, 142–45. The quotation is in Chester, *Embattled Maiden*, p. 52.

59. For Dickinson's later political activities, see Chester, *Embattled Maiden*, chaps. 8, 13.

60. Venet, *Neither Ballots nor Bullets*, pp. 129–30; Massey, *Bonnet Brigades*, pp. 158–59. The quotations are on p. 159.

CHAPTER 4

1. On the postwar suffrage struggle, see Ellen C. DuBois, *Feminism and Suffrage: The Emergence of an Independent Women's Movement in America, 1848–1869* (Ithaca, N.Y., 1978); Eleanor Flexner, *Century of Struggle: The Woman's Rights Movement in the United States*, rev. ed. (Cambridge, 1975), chap. 10; Kathleen Barry, *Susan B. Anthony: A Biography* (New York, 1988), chap. 7.

2. Alma Lutz, *Susan B. Anthony: Rebel, Crusader, Humanitarian* (Boston, 1959), pp. 147–48; Charles C. Coleman, *Election of 1868* (New York, 1933), p. 197.

3. Horace Bushnell, *Women's Suffrage: The Reform Against Nature* (New York, 1869), pp. 138, 141.

4. Elizabeth Cady Stanton et al., eds. *History of Woman Suffrage*, 6 vols. (Rochester and New York, 1881–1922), 2: 304–5.

5. Ibid., 2: 551.

6. Alice H. Sokoloff, *Kate Chase for the Defense* (New York, 1971), pp. 140–50; Frederick J. Blue, *Salmon Chase: A Life in Politics* (Kent, Ohio, 1987), pp. 292–97.

7. *The Personal Memoirs of Julia Dent Grant*, ed. by John Y. Simon (New York, 1975), p. 171.

8. Mrs. John A. [Mary] Logan, *The Part Taken by Women in American History* (Wilmington, Del., 1912; reprint New York, 1972), pp. 1–17; "Mary Logan," in *NAW*, 2: 421–22; *Chicago Tribune*, October 5, 1884.

9. Stanton et al., *History of Woman Suffrage*, 4: 572–73; *Woman's Journal*, March 9, 1872.

10. Louise R. Noun, *Strong-Minded Women: The Emergence of the Woman Suffrage Movement in Iowa* (Ames, Ia., 1969), pp. 125–27; *Woman's Journal*, May 13, 1876.

11. Stanton et al., *History of Woman Suffrage*, 2: 180–81.

12. On Victoria Woodhull, see Johanna Johnston, *Mrs. Satan: The Incredible Saga of Victoria Woodhull* (New York, 1967); Emanie Sachs, *The Terrible Siren: Victoria Woodhull* (New York, 1928).

13. Victoria Woodhull, Speech to the National Woman Suffrage Convention, May 11, 1871, in Paulina W. Davis, *A History of the National Woman's Rights Movement* (New York, 1871, reprint 1971), pp. 115–16; Stanton et al., *History of Woman Suffrage*, 2: 518–19.

14. Stanton et al., *History of Woman Suffrage*, 2: 519.

15. Ibid., 2: 519–20.

16. Quoted in Israel Kugler, *From Ladies to Women: The Organized Struggle for Woman's Rights in the Reconstruction Era* (Westport, Conn., 1987), p. 111.

17. Stanton et al., *History of Woman Suffrage*, 2: 520.

18. *Woman's Journal*, October 5, 12, November 2, 9, 1872.

19. Ibid., September 21, 1872; *New York Times*, October 8, 1872.

20. Giraud Chester, *Embattled Maiden: The Life of Anna Dickinson* (New York, 1951), chap. 8; *New York Tribune*, October 26, 1872.

21. Harriet H. Robinson, *Massachusetts in the Woman Suffrage Movement* (Boston, 1881), pp. 76–77.

22. *Woman's Journal*, September 13, 1884.

23. Quoted in Lori D. Ginzberg, *Women and the Work of Benevolence: Morality, Politics, and Class in the Nineteenth-Century United States* (New Haven, Conn., 1990), p. 185.

24. *Woman's Journal*, September 30, 1876.

25. Ibid., August 7, 1880.

26. Quoted in Elinor R. Hays, *Morning Star: A Biography of Lucy Stone* (New York, 1961), pp. 280–81.

27. Quoted in Leslie Wheeler, ed., *Loving Warriors: Selected Letters of Lucy Stone and Henry B. Blackwell, 1853 to 1893* (New York, 1981), p. 286.

28. Rheta C. Dorr, *Susan B. Anthony: The Woman Who Changed the Mind of a Nation* (New York, 1928), pp. 285–88.

29. Quoted in Lutz, *Anthony*, p. 243.

30. *Woman's Journal*, October 22, 1892, October 10, 1896. See also Lynn Sherr, *Failure is Impossible: Susan B. Anthony in Her Own Words* (New York, 1995), pp. 103–5.

31. Ibid., September 22, 1888, October 10, 1896; *Chicago Tribune*, September 23, 1900; *Boston Evening Transcript*, September 11, 1888.

32. See the essay on Lockwood in Madeleine Stern, *We the Women* (New York, 1963), esp. pp. 222–26.

33. *Boston Evening Transcript*, October 21, 24, 1884.

34. Quoted in Stern, *We the Women*, p. 226.

35. *Boston Evening Transcript*, September 24, October 17, 1888.

36. See "A Minnesota Farm Woman in Politics," in Gerda Lerner, ed., *The Female Experience: An American Documentary* (Indianapolis, Ind., 1977), pp. 361–73.

37. *Woman's Journal*, September 23, October 28, 1876, September 18, 1880.

38. *Woman's Column*, February 8, 1890.

39. James Bryce, *The American Commonwealth*, 3d ed., (New York, 1894), 2: 208.

40. Chandler's comment is cited in Matthew Josephson, *The Politicos, 1865–1896* (New York, 1938), pp. 139–40.

41. *Chicago Tribune*, October 1, 1880.

42. Paula C. Baker, *The Moral Frameworks of Public Life: Gender, Politics, and the State in Rural New York, 1870–1930* (New York, 1991); *New York Times*, October 1, 7, 1892.

43. *Chicago Tribune*, September 1, 1880. See also ibid., September 24, October 2, 4, 1880, October 20, 1884.

44. *Woman's Journal*, September 18, 1880.

45. *Chicago Tribune*, September 25, 29, 1880.

46. For the life of Nellie Blinn, see her obituary in the *San Francisco Chronicle*, July 5, 1909. Her part in Republican campaigns is mentioned in the *Chicago Tribune*, September 12, 1884.

47. For Clara Shortridge Foltz, see *NAW*, 1: 641–43.

48. *New York Times*, October 18, 1895.

49. George C. Rable, *Civil Wars: Women and the Crisis of Southern Nationalism* (Urbana, Ill., 1989), p. 230.

50. Eric Foner, *Reconstruction, 1863–1877* (New York, 1987), pp. 290–91.

51. Rebecca Latimer Felton, *Country Life in Georgia* (Atlanta, 1919; reprint New York, 1980), pp. 119–21. See also John E. Talmadge, *Rebecca Latimer Felton* (Athens, Ga., 1960), pp. 36–62.

CHAPTER 5

1. Jack S. Blocker, Jr. *"Give to the Winds Thy Fears": The Women's Temperance Crusade, 1873–1874* (Westport, Conn., 1985), pp. 169–70, 192–93, 194–95, 210.

2. Ruth Bordin, *Women and Temperance: The Quest for Power and Liberty, 1873–1900* (Philadelphia, 1981), esp. chap. 7; Barbara L. Epstein, *The Politics of Domesticity: Women, Evangelism, and Temperance in Nineteenth-Century America* (Middletown, Conn., 1981), chap. 5.

3. Bordin, *Women and Temperance*, pp. 95–96, 118–19; Epstein, *Politics of Domesticity*, pp. 120–23.

4. Paul Kleppner, "The Greenback and Prohibition Parties," in Arthur M. Schlesinger, Jr., ed., *History of U.S. Political Parties* (New York, 1973), 2: 1549–81; Epstein, *Politics of Domesticity*, p. 122.

5. Bordin, *Women and Temperance*, pp. 124–25.

6. Ibid., pp. 127–28; Frances Willard, *Glimpses of Fifty Years: The Autobiography of an American Woman* (Chicago, 1889; reprint New York, 1970), p. 439.

7. Bordin, *Women and Temperance*, p. 128.

8. Quoted in Alphonso A. Hopkins, *The Life of Clinton Bowen Fisk* (New York, 1888), p. 190.

9. *Boston Evening Transcript*, September 12, 1888.

10. Bordin, *Women and Temperance*, pp. 132–33.

11. Israel Kugler, *From Ladies to Women: The Organized Struggle for Woman's Rights in the Reconstruction Era* (Westport, Conn., 1987), pp. 115–56; Kleppner, "The Greenback and Prohibition Parties"; *Woman's Journal*, October 25, 1884.

12. Julie R. Jeffrey, "Women in the Southern Farmers' Alliance," *Feminist Studies* 3 (Fall 1975): 72–91.

13. Douglas Bakken, ed., "Luna E. Kellie and the Farmers' Alliance," *Nebraska History* 50 (Summer 1969): 184–205.

14. "Sarah Van DeVort Emery," in *NAW*, 1: 582; Pauline Adams and Emma S. Thornton, *A Populist Assault: Sarah E. Van DeVort Emery on American Democracy, 1862–1895* (Bowling Green, Ohio, 1982).

15. "Annie Diggs," in ibid., 1: 481–82.

16. Richard Stiller, *Queen of the Populists: The Story of Mary Lease* (New York, 1970); D. R. Blumberg, "Mary E. Lease, Populist Orator: A Profile," *Kansas History* 1 (Spring 1978): 3–15.

17. Barton C. Shaw, *The Wool Hat Boys: Georgia's Populist Party* (Baton Rouge, La., 1984), pp. 76–77.

18. Beverly Beeton, *Women Vote in the West: The Woman Suffrage Movement, 1869–1896* (New York, 1986), pp. 111–13; James E. Wright, *The Politics of Populism: Dissent in Colorado* (New Haven, Conn., 1974), pp. 198–99.

19. Beeton, *Women Vote in the West*, pp. 125–29.

20. Mari Jo Buhle, *Women and American Socialism, 1870–1920* (Urbana, Ill., 1981); Ira Kipnis, *The American Socialist Movement* (New York, 1952), pp. 260–65.

21. Buhle, *Women and American Socialism*, p. 145.

22. Willard, *Glimpses of Fifty Years*, p. 439; *Woman's Journal*, September 15, 1888.

23. Giraud Chester, *Embattled Maiden: The Life of Anna Dickinson* (New York, 1951), pp. 238–52.

24. *Woman's Journal*, September 17, 1892.

25. Ibid., September 1, 1888; *Boston Evening Transcript*, September 4, 1888.

26. Quoted in essay on J. Ellen Foster in Elmer C. Adams and Warren D. Foster, *Heroines of Modern Progress* (New York, 1913), pp. 268–69.

27. Quoted in Paula C. Baker, *The Moral Frameworks of Public Life: Gender, Politics, and the State in Rural New York, 1870–1930* (New York, 1991), p. 84.

28. *Boston Evening Transcript*, September 16, 1892; *New York Herald*, September 17, 1892.

29. *Woman's Journal*, September 19, 1908.

30. *New York Times*, October 18, 1895.

31. *Chicago Tribune*, October 27, 1904.

32. *Woman's Journal*, October 10, 1896.

33. Ibid., October 17, 24, 1896.

34. Ibid., June 18, 1898.

35. Elizabeth Cady Stanton et al., eds., *History of Woman Suffrage*, 6 vols. (Rochester and New York, 1881–1922), 4: 436–37.

36. Ibid., 4: 437; *Woman's Journal*, October 29, 1892.

37. Quoted in George H. Knoles, *The Presidential Campaign and Election of 1892* (Stanford, Calif., 1942), p. 136.

38. Stanley L. Jones, *The Presidential Election of 1896* (Madison, Wis., 1964), pp. 87–89, 329–30.

39. Quoted in Robert F. Durden, *The Climax of Populism: The Election of 1896* (Lexington, Ky., 1965), p. 83.

40. Louis Koenig, *Bryan: A Political Biography* (New York, 1971), pp. 236–37.

41. Quoted in Betty Boyd Caroli, *First Ladies* (New York, 1987), pp. 114–15.

42. Quoted in *Woman's Column*, January 2, 1897.

43. Quoted in ibid.

CHAPTER 6

1. A list of the states adopting "school suffrage" appears in Mildred Adams et al., *How We Won It* (New York, 1940), pp. 165–66. A few states also allowed women to vote on tax and bond measures. There is no full study of partial suffrage. For a brief statement on the subject, see Eleanor Flexner, *Century of Struggle: The Woman's Rights Movement in the United States*, rev. ed. (Cambridge, Mass., 1975), pp. 176–77.

2. Lois B. Merk, "Boston's Historic Public School Crisis," *New England Quarterly* 31 (June 1958): 172–99. For the voter turnout figures in Table 1, see *Woman's Journal*, September 17, 1904; *Boston Evening Transcript*, December 12, 1888.

3. *New York Times*, April 8, 1889.

4. Ibid.; *Woman's Column*, April 19, 1890; *Woman's Journal* April 24, 1897, March 21, 1903; *Woman Suffrage: Arguments and Results, 1910–1911* (New York, 1911; reprint 1971), p. 38.

5. Rosalind U. Moss, "The 'Girls' from Syracuse: Sex Role Negotiations of Kansas Women in Politics, 1887–1890," in Susan Armitage and Elizabeth Jameson, eds., *The Women's West* (Norman, Okla., 1987), pp. 253–64. The quotation is on p. 257.

6. Wallace Smith, "The Birth of Petticoat Government," *American History Illustrated* 10 (May 1984): 50–55; *Woman's Journal*, July 22, 1899.

7. The best study of female enfranchisement in the first four western states is Beverly Beeton, *Women Vote in the West: The Woman Suffrage Movement, 1869–1896* (New York, 1986).

8. Quoted in Elizabeth Cady Stanton et al., *History of Woman Suffrage*, 6 vols. (New York and Rochester, 1881–1922), 4: 995.

9. Ibid., 4: 1009–10. One may question the legitimacy of the voting statistics presented in this chapter, as they come from pro-suffrage publications such as the *Woman's Journal* and *History of Woman Suffrage* and cannot be easily corroborated. However, these figures were cited over and over again in the suffragist literature and, to my knowledge, never once disputed by anyone in the anti-suffrage movement.

10. Stanton et al., *History of Woman Suffrage*, 4: 594–95; *Woman's Column*, August 7, 1897, October 8, 1898.

11. Stanton et al., *History of Woman Suffrage*, 4: 951–53. A complete county-by-county breakdown is given on p. 952. See also *Woman's Journal*, June 30, November 3, 1900. The quotation can be found in ibid., November 14, 1896.

12. Helen L. Sumner [Woodbury], *Equal Suffrage* (New York, 1909; reprint 1972), pp. 97–103. A table of the votes in nine counties for 1906 appears on p. 103.

13. Quoted in ibid., pp. xx; see also pp. 45, 47, 118–19. For a discussion of independent voting in Colorado in these years, see *New York Times*, November 16, 1902.

14. Sumner, *Equal Suffrage*, p. 146.

15. Ibid., p. 50.

16. Ibid., pp. 130–31.

17. Quoted in ibid., pp. 63, 64.

18. Ibid., p. 82. See also *Woman's Journal*, April 14, 1900.

19. Grover Cleveland, "Would Woman Suffrage Be Unwise?" *Ladies Home Journal* 22 (October 1905): 7–8.

20. Quoted in Beeton, *Women Vote in the West*, p. 136.

21. Quoted in Sumner, *Equal Suffrage*, p. 69.

22. *Chicago Tribune*, September 13, 1904.

23. Ibid.; *New York Times*, November 9, 1904.

24. *Woman's Journal*, October 27, 1900.

25. *Chicago Tribune*, September 16, October 21, 1900.

26. *Woman's Journal*, November 10, 1900.

27. Michael E. McGerr, *The Decline of Popular Politics: The American North, 1865–1928* (New York, 1986); Richard J. Jensen, *The Winning of the Midwest: Social and Political Conflict, 1888–1896* (Chicago, 1971). The quotation is from McGerr, "Political Style and Women's Power, 1830–1930," *Journal of American History* 77 (December 1990): 870.

28. Maureen A. Flanagan, "Gender and Urban Political Reform: The City Club and the Woman's City Club of Chicago in the Progressive Era," *American Historical Review* 95 (October 1990): 1032–50.

29. Allen F. Davis, *American Heroine: The Life and Legend of Jane Addams* (New York, 1973), pp. 121–25; John C. Farrell, *Beloved Lady: A History of Jane Addams' Ideas on Reform and Peace* (Baltimore, 1967), pp. 75–77.

30. The anti-Tammany struggle is described in S. Sara Monoson, "The Lady and the Tiger: Women's Electoral Activism in New York City Before Suffrage," *Journal of Women's History* 2 (Fall 1990): 100–35.

31. Ibid., pp. 106–10. For the work done by the West End Club, see "New York Women in Politics," in *Woman's Journal*, November 3, 1900.

32. Quoted in *Woman's Column*, October 16, 1897.

33. Quoted in ibid., October 2, 1897.

34. *Woman's Journal*, November 10, 1901.

35. Ibid., March 8, 1902.

36. Monoson, "Lady and the Tiger," pp. 120–23.

37. *Woman's Journal*, November 11, 1905.

38. Robert M. LaFollette, *Autobiography* (Madison, Wis., 1913), pp. 312–13.

39. S. J. Duncan-Clark, *The Progressive Movement* (Boston, 1913; reprint New York, 1972), p. 90.

40. *Chicago Tribune*, September 24, 1912.

41. On Ruth McCormick, see Kristi Miller, *Ruth Hanna McCormick: A Life in Politics* (Albuquerque, N.M., 1991); on Frances Kellor, see Ellen Fitzpatrick, *Endless Crusade: Women Social Scientists and Progressive Reform* (New York, 1990), pp. 146–57.

42. Mrs. J. Borden Harriman, *From Pinafores to Politics* (New York, 1923), esp. pp. 111–25. The quotation is on p. 121.

43. Blanche W. Cook, *Eleanor Roosevelt*, vol. 1: 1884–1933 (New York, 1992), chap. 8. The quotation is on p. 190.

44. *Woman Suffrage: Arguments and Results*, pp. 24, 28, 31, 33.

45. Frances M. Bjorkman and Annie Porritt, comp., *Woman Suffrage: History, Arguments, and Results* (New York, 1917), pp. 49, 53; *New York Times*, November 6, 1912; George Creel, "What Have Women Done with the Vote?" *Century Magazine* 87 (March 1914): 663–71.

46. Bjorkman and Porritt, *Woman Suffrage*, pp. 58, 63, 68, 69; Michael P. Malone and Richard B. Roeder, *Montana: A History of Two Centuries* (Seattle, 1976), pp. 203–4.

47. Joel H. Goldstein, *The Effects of the Adoption of Woman Suffrage: Sex Differences in Voting Behavior—Illinois, 1914–21* (New York, 1984); Fred W. Eckert, "Effects of Woman Suffrage on the Political Situation in the City of Chicago," *Political Science Quarterly* 31 (March 1916): 105–21.

48. William F. Ogburn and Inez Goltra, "How Women Vote," *Political Science Quarterly* 34 (September 1919): 413–33.

CHAPTER 7

1. The first part of this chapter is based especially on the following works: Aileen S. Kraditor, T*he Ideas of the Woman Suffrage Movement, 1890–1920* (New York, 1965); David Morgan, *Suffragists and Democrats: The Politics of Woman Suffrage in America* (East Lansing, Mich., 1972), chap. 6; Inez Irwin, *The Story of the Woman's Party* (New York, 1921; reprint 1971).

2. Quoted in Morgan, *Suffragists and Democrats*, pp. 93–94. A slightly different strategy, opposing specific anti-suffrage legislators, had already been pursued on a statewide basis. See Sharon H. Strom, "Leadership and Tactics in the American Woman Suffrage Movement: A New Perspective from Massachusetts," *Journal of American History* 62 (September 1975): 314.

3. Irwin, *Woman's Party*, pp. 73–86; Kraditor, *Woman Suffrage*, pp. 192–94; Morgan, *Suffragists and Democrats*, pp. 93–94.

4. Loretta Zimmerman, "Alice Paul and the National Woman's Party, 1912–1920," Ph.D. Dissertation, Tulane University, 1964, pp. 204–9; Irwin, *Woman's Party*, pp. 172–80; *Chicago Tribune*, November 7, 1916, p. 3.

5. *New York Times*, August 5, 7, 12, 1916; *Woman's Journal*, August 12, 1916.

6. *Chicago Tribune*, September 8, 1916; *Literary Digest* 53 (October 28, 1916): 1087; *San Francisco Chronicle*, October 19, 1916. J. Leonard Bates and Vanette M. Schwartz, "Golden Special Campaign Train: Republican Women Campaign for Charles Evans Hughes for President in 1916," *Montana* 37 (Summer 1987): 26–35, offers a very useful, though overly favorable, view of the event.

7. *New York Times*, October 12, 1916.

8. Ibid., November 5, 1916.

9. Zimmerman, "Alice Paul," pp. 214–16.

10. "Jeannette Rankin," in *NAW*, 4: 566–68; see also her oral history, "Activist for World Peace, Women's Rights, and Democratic Government," Bancroft Library, University of California, Berkeley.

11. Anne Bail Howard, *The Long Campaign: A Biography of Anne Martin* (Reno, Nev., 1985), esp. chap. 8.

12. *New York Times*, November 10, 1917; *Woman Citizen*, July 27, September 14, November 16, 1918.

13. *Woman Citizen*, March 30, June 8, July 20, 1918.

14. Morgan, *Suffragists and Democrats*, pp. 129–33; Irwin, *Woman's Party*, pp. 380–83.

15. Gene Smith, *When the Cheering Stopped: The Last Years of Woodrow Wilson* (New York, 1964); Judith L. Weaver, "Edith Bolling Wilson as First Lady: A Study in the Power of Personality, 1919–1920," *Presidential Studies Quarterly* 15 (Winter 1985): 51–76.

16. On women as convention delegates, see Sophonisba Breckinridge, *Women in the Twentieth Century* (New York, 1933), pp. 275–78.

17. For women on party committees, see ibid., pp. 279–82. For Democratic party emphasis on its "fifty-fifty plan," see ads in *Woman Citizen*, September 11, 25, 1920.

18. J. Stanley Lemons, *The Woman Citizen: Social Feminism in the 1920s* (Urbana, Ill., 1973), pp. 87–89; *San Francisco Chronicle*, September 21, 23, 25, October 1, 1920; *Chicago Tribune*, September 23, 1920.

19. Lemons, *Woman Citizen*, pp. 87–97; Randolph C. Downes, *The Rise of Warren Gamaliel Harding, 1865–1920* (Columbus, Ohio, 1970), p. 510. See also "Which Party Did It?" *Woman Citizen*, September 18, 1920.

20. Sara Alpern and Dale Baum, "Female Ballots: The Impact of the Nineteenth Amendment," *Journal of Interdisciplinary History* 16 (Summer 1985): 43–67. In Courtney Brown, *Ballots of Tumult: A Portrait of Volatility in American Voting* (Ann Arbor, Mich., 1991), chap. 6, the author argues that the Republicans must have made greater

efforts to recruit women voters in 1920 than their opponents since the GOP totals that year were much higher than in 1916, unlike the Democratic totals.

21. Lemons, *Woman Citizen*, pp. 87–89. On the situation in one state, see Carole Nichols, *Votes and More for Women: Suffrage and After in Connecticut* (New York, 1983), esp. pp. 33–35.

22. Charles E. Russell, "Is Woman Suffrage a Failure?" *Century Magazine* 107 (March 1924): 724–30; Nancy Schoonmaker, "Where Does She Stand?" ibid., 113 (January 1927): 355.

23. The following analysis is based in part on several works including: William Chafe, *The American Woman, 1920–1970* (New York, 1972), chap. 1; William L. O'Neill, *Everyone Was Brave* (Chicago, 1969), chap. 9; Dorothy M. Brown, *Setting a Course: American Women in the 1920s* (Boston, 1987), chap. 3; Felice Gordon, *After Winning: The Legacy of the New Jersey Suffragists, 1920–1947* (New Brunswick, N.J., 1986); and Lemons, *Woman Citizen*.

24. Quoted in Ernestine Evans, "Women in the Washington Scene," *Century Magazine* 106 (August 1923): 508.

25. Michael McGerr, "Political Style and Women's Power, 1830–1930," *Journal of American History* 77 (December 1990): 882–84.

26. Robert S. Lynd and Helen M. Lynd, *Middletown* (New York, 1929), p. 420.

27. Louise M. Young, *In the Public Interest: The League of Women Voters, 1920–1970* (New York, 1989).

28. Anne Martin, "Feminists and Future Political Action," *The Nation* 120 (February 3, 1925): 185–86.

29. For the plight of Alice Paul and the National Woman's party, see Nancy F. Cott, *The Grounding of Modern Feminism* (New Haven, Conn., 1987).

30. Data are compiled from Breckinridge, *Women in the Twentieth Century*, pp. 249–51; Marguerite M. Wells, "Some Effects of Woman Suffrage," *Annals* 143 (May 1929): 207; Anne F. Scott, *The Southern Lady: From Pedestal to Politics, 1830–1930* (Chicago, 1970), p. 201.

31. Wells, "Some Effects of Woman Suffrage," pp. 207–10.

32. Sarah Butler, "After Ten Years," *Woman Citizen* (April 1931): 11.

33. On Moscowitz, see Elisabeth Israels Perry, *Belle Moscowitz: Feminine Politics and the Exercise of Power in the Age of Alfred E. Smith* (New York, 1987). For the political acts of Willebrandt, see Dorothy M. Brown, *Mabel Walker Willebrandt: A Study of Power, Loyalty, and Law* (Knoxville, Tenn., 1984), chap. 6.

34. For women's role in partisan politics between 1930 and 1960, see Susan Ware, *Beyond Suffrage: Women in the New Deal* (Cambridge, Mass., 1981); Susan M. Hartmann, *The Home Front and Beyond: American Women in the 1940s* (Boston, 1982), chap. 8; Marguerite J. Fisher, "Women in the Political Parties," *Annals* 251 (May 1947): 87–93; and Eugenia Kaledin, *Mothers and More: American Women in the 1950s* (Boston, 1984), chap. 5.

Bibliographic Essay

A study of women in partisan politics before the suffrage amendment is no easy task, for there are no general works on the subject. It therefore becomes necessary to consult a wide variety of primary and secondary sources in order to cull out needed pieces of information. Most important among the available primary materials are the abundant collections of daily and weekly newspapers from the pre–1920 period, whose issues occasionally contain items of great interest regarding women's partisan political activities. For the half-century after 1870, the best newspaper source is the *Woman's Journal*, edited by suffragists Lucy Stone and her husband Henry Blackwell, and subsequently by their daughter Alice Stone Blackwell. For several years, Ms. Blackwell also edited the *Woman's Column*, a similar publication. Although both were concerned mainly with woman suffrage, there are often valuable references to partisan political matters, especially during presidential election years. In addition to newspapers, certain collections of contemporary documents and commentary provide significant material. Most notable is the multivolume account of the woman suffrage movement edited by Elizabeth Cady Stanton, Susan B. Anthony, Matilda J. Gage, and Ida H. Harper, *A History of Woman Suffrage* (Rochester and New York, 1881–1922). Also revealing are the various manuals put out by the suffrage groups such as Frances M. Bjorkman and Annie Porritt, comp., *Woman Suffrage: History, Arguments, and Results* (New York, 1917). However, some of the contents of these publications may be biased and must be used with caution.

Besides newspapers and collections of documents and commentaries, the diaries, journals, and letters of prominent women in the pre–1920 years are sometimes very useful. Among the best examples are Margaret Bayard Smith, *The First Forty Years of Washington Society*, edited by Gaillard Hunt (New York, 1906; reprint 1965), *Lydia Maria Child: Selected Letters, 1817–1880*, edited by Milton Meltzer and Patricia G. Holland (Amherst, Mass., 1982), and *Elizabeth Cady Stanton, As Revealed in Her Letters, Diary, and Reminiscences*, 2 vols., edited by Theodore Stanton and Harriot Stanton Blatch (New York, 1922). Biographical and autobiographical works are also significant. Frances Willard, *Glimpses of Fifty Years: The Autobiography of an American Woman* (Chicago, 1889; reprint New York, 1970), and Rebecca Latimer Felton, *Country Life in Georgia* (Atlanta, 1919; reprint, New York, 1980), contain a number of revealing items. Pamela Herr's *Jessie Benton Frémont* (New York, 1987) and Jean H. Baker's *Mary Lincoln: A Biography* (New York, 1987) are particularly helpful in depicting the role of nineteenth-century politician's wives in promoting their husband's career. Well-researched, shorter biographical sketches of many prominent female political figures can be found in Edward T. James, Janet W. James, and Paul S. Boyer, eds., *Notable American Women, 1607–1950*, 3 vols. (Cambridge, Mass., 1971). Also useful for the activities of presidential wives is Betty Boyd Caroli, *First Ladies* (New York, 1987) and Carl S. Anthony, *First Ladies: The Saga of the Presidents' Wives and Their Power*, 2 vols. (New York, 1990).

Among general secondary works, a pioneering essay on women in the political sphere is Louise M. Young, "Women's Place in American Politics: The Historical Perspective," *Journal of Politics* 38 (August 1976): 295–335. A more recent and highly sophisticated attempt to locate women's place in the pre-suffrage political world is Paula Baker, "The Domestication of Politics: Women and American Political Society, 1780–1920," *American Historical Review* 89 (June 1984): 620–47. Although she slights the connection with partisan politics, Baker provides an excellent introduction to women's involvement in other forms of political activity. Offering to some degree a corrective to Baker's essay is Lori D. Ginzberg's thoroughly researched volume *Women and the Work of Benevolence: Morality, Politics, and Class in the Nineteenth-Century United States* (New Haven, Conn., 1990), which shows how women's attachment to reform eventually led them to pursue partisan goals. Women's growing public role in the nineteenth century, which at times included partisan activity, is also the theme of Mary P. Ryan, *Women in Public: Between Banners and Ballots, 1825–1880* (Baltimore, 1990). A survey covering a broader period of time, though based mainly on secondary sources, is

Glenna Mathews, *The Rise of Public Woman* (New York, 1992). Michael McGerr, "Political Style and Women's Power, 1830–1930," *Journal of American History* 77 (December 1990): 864–95, is another important study of the changing nature of women's political participation from the last century to this one.

Little has been written about women's place in public life during the colonial period, partly because of the limitations on such experience. Robert J. Dinkin, *Voting in Provincial America: A Study of Elections in the Thirteen British Colonies, 1689–1776* (Westport, Conn., 1977), describes the restrictions on women voting but presents a few examples of other forms of political participation in that era. Women's emerging public role in the latter part of the eighteenth century is thoroughly discussed in Mary Beth Norton, *Liberty's Daughters: The Revolutionary Experience of American Women, 1750–1800* (Boston, 1980), and from a somewhat different angle in Linda K. Kerber, *Women of the Republic: Intellect and Ideology in Revolutionary America* (Chapel Hill, N.C., 1980). Kerber dwells especially on the theme of "Republican motherhood" as an alternative to an openly partisan role in post-Revolutionary politics. Kerber and Norton see greater gains for women in these years than Joan Hoff-Wilson does in her essay "The Illusion of Change: Women and the American Revolution," in Alfred F. Young, ed., *The American Revolution: Explorations in the History of American Radicalism* (DeKalb, Ill., 1976). A lot has been written about Abigail Adams, the most frequently quoted female figure of the time. For a recent summary, see Edith B. Gelles, "The Abigail Industry," *William and Mary Quarterly*, 3d ser., 45 (October 1988): 656–83. Some references to other women in politics in the post-Revolutionary period can be found in Janet W. James, *Changing Ideas about Women in the United States, 1776–1825* (New York, 1981).

There is no general study of women's partisan activities in the Early National period, though one can get an overview of their nonpartisan activities in Anne M. Boylan, "Women and Politics in the Era Before Seneca Falls," *Journal of the Early Republic* 10 (Fall 1990): 364–82. A few references to partisan activities can be found in David H. Fischer, *The Revolution of American Conservatism: The Federalist Party in the Era of Jeffersonian Democracy* (New York, 1965), and in Judith A. Klinghoffer and Lois Elkis, " 'The Petticoat Electors': Women's Suffrage in New Jersey, 1776–1807," *Journal of the Early Republic* 12 (Summer 1992): 159–93. Although focusing largely on reform, women's entry into partisan politics in the middle decades of the nineteenth century is discussed in the previously cited book by Lori Ginzberg, *Women and the Work of Benevolence*, and in her essay " 'Moral Suasion Is Moral Balderdash': Women,

Politics, and Social Activism in the 1850s," *Journal of American History* 73 (December 1986): 601–22. Dealing more directly with certain aspects of partisan activity are Jayne Crumpler DeFiore, "COME, and Bring the Ladies: Tennessee Women and the Politics of Opportunity during the Presidential Campaigns of 1840 and 1844," *Tennessee Historical Quarterly* 51 (Winter 1992): 197–212; Jean G. Hales, " 'Co-Laborers in the Cause': Women in the Antebellum Nativist Movement," *Civil War History* 25 (June 1979): 119–38; and Wendy Hamand Venet, *Neither Ballots nor Bullets: Women Abolitionists and the Civil War* (Charlottesville, Va., 1991). George C. Rable, *Civil Wars: Women and the Crisis of Southern Nationalism* (Urbana, Ill., 1989), examines the political role of women in the South.

For the post–Civil War era, several works focusing primarily on the woman suffrage movement furnish important background material regarding partisan politics. These include Ellen C. DuBois, *Feminism and Suffrage: The Emergence of an Independent Women's Movement in America, 1848–1869* (Ithaca, N.Y., 1978); Eleanor Flexner, *Century of Struggle: The Woman's Rights Movement in the United States*, rev. ed. (Cambridge, Mass., 1975); Kathleen Barry, *Susan B. Anthony: A Biography* (New York, 1988); and Israel Kugler, *From Ladies to Women: The Organized Struggle for Woman's Rights in the Reconstruction Era* (Westport, Conn., 1987), as well as the previously cited books by Ginzberg and Ryan. For women and the temperance movement, see Ruth Bordin, *Women and Temperance: The Quest for Power and Liberty, 1873–1900* (Philadelphia, 1981), and Barbara L. Epstein, *The Politics of Domesticity: Women, Evangelism, and Temperance in Nineteenth-Century America* (Middletown, Conn., 1981). Late nineteenth-century rural women's link with the public sphere is the subject of Paula C. Baker, *The Moral Frameworks of Public Life: Gender, Politics, and the State in Rural New York, 1870–1930* (New York, 1991). Populist women are discussed in Julie R. Jeffrey, "Women in the Southern Farmers' Alliance," *Feminist Studies* 3 (Fall 1975): 72–91, Douglas Bakken, ed., "Luna E. Kellie and the Farmers' Alliance," *Nebraska History* 50 (Summer 1969): 184–205, and Richard Stiller, *Queen of the Populists: The Story of Mary Lease* (New York, 1970). Mari Jo Buhle, *Women and American Socialism, 1870–1920* (Urbana, Ill., 1981), is an excellent study of women's connection with socialism.

On the subject of female enfranchisement in the early western states, the best study is Beverly Beeton, *Women Vote in the West: The Woman Suffrage Movement, 1869–1896* (New York, 1986). An excellent contemporary analysis of women voting at the turn of the century in Colorado is Helen L. Sumner [Woodbury], *Equal Suffrage* (New York, 1909; reprint

1972). The political impact of nonvoting women in that same time period can be seen in S. Sara Monoson, "The Lady and the Tiger: Women's Electoral Activism in New York City before Suffrage," *Journal of Women's History* 2 (Fall 1990): 100–35, and Maureen A. Flanagan, "Gender and Urban Political Reform: The City Club and the Women's City Club of Chicago in the Progressive Era," *American Historical Review* 95 (October 1990): 1032–50. The connection between partisan politics and the final drive for woman's suffrage is explored in David Morgan, *Suffragists and Democrats: The Politics of Woman Suffrage in America* (East Lansing, Mich., 1972), Aileen S. Kraditor, *The Ideas of the Woman Suffrage Movement, 1890–1920* (New York, 1965), Inez Irwin, *The Story of the Woman's Party* (New York, 1921; reprint 1971), J. Stanley Lemons, *The Woman Citizen: Social Feminism in the 1920s* (Urbana, Ill., 1973), and Nancy F. Cott, *The Grounding of Modern Feminism* (New Haven, Conn., 1987). The last two titles are also significant for understanding the early post-suffrage years of the 1920s.

Index

About the Author

ROBERT J. DINKIN is Professor of History at California State University. He is the author of *Voting in Provincial America* (Greenwood, 1977), *Voting in Revolutionary America* (Greenwood, 1982), and *Campaigning in America* (Greenwood, 1989).

ISBN 0-313-29482-8

90000>

EAN

9 780313 294822

HARDCOVER BAR CODE